THE WORKS OF

WITTER BYNNER

GENERAL EDITOR, JAMES KRAFT

SELECTED POEMS
*Edited, and with a critical introduction, by Richard Wilbur;
biographical introduction by James Kraft*

LIGHT VERSE AND SATIRES
Edited, and with an introduction, by William Jay Smith

THE CHINESE TRANSLATIONS

THE JADE MOUNTAIN
Introduction by Burton Watson

THE WAY OF LIFE ACCORDING TO LAOTZU
Introduction by David Lattimore

PROSE PIECES
Edited, and with an introduction, by James Kraft

LETTERS
Edited, and with an introduction, by James Kraft

LIGHT VERSE AND SATIRES

PHOTOGRAPH OF WITTER BYNNER
IN SANTA FE, MARCH 1930,
BY ALFRED A. KNOPF

THE WORKS OF
WITTER BYNNER

GENERAL EDITOR, JAMES KRAFT

LIGHT VERSE AND SATIRES

EDITED, AND WITH
AN INTRODUCTION, BY

William Jay Smith

FARRAR · STRAUS · GIROUX / NEW YORK

Copyright © 1978 by The Witter Bynner Foundation
Copyright © 1919, 1920, 1925, 1926, 1929, 1933,
1935, 1940, 1947, 1960 by Witter Bynner
Copyright renewed 1947, 1948, 1953, 1954, 1957, 1961,
1962, 1967, 1968 by Witter Bynner
Copyright renewed 1974 by The Executors
of the Estate of Witter Bynner
The original Spectra reprinted by permission of
The Witter Bynner Foundation,
and Mrs. Stanhope B. Ficke;
later poems by "Emanuel Morgan"
copyright © 1961 by Witter Bynner;
later poems by "Anne Knish"
copyright © 1961 by Mrs. Gladys Ficke;
poems by "Elijah Hay"
copyright © 1961 by Mrs. Marjorie Allen Seiffert
All rights reserved
First printing, 1978
Printed in the United States of America
Published simultaneously in Canada by
McGraw-Hill Ryerson Ltd., Toronto
Designed by Cynthia Krupat

Quotations from The Letters of D. H. Lawrence,
used by permission of the Estate of
Mrs. Frieda Lawrence, Laurence Pollinger Ltd.,
and The Viking Press, Inc.

Library of Congress Cataloging in Publication Data
Bynner, Witter, 1881–1968.
Light verse and satires.
(The works of Witter Bynner)
1. Title. II. Series: Bynner, Witter, 1881–1968.
PS3503.Y45L48   1977   811'.5'2   77–11158

This book is published with the aid of a grant from
The Witter Bynner Foundation for Poetry

Editorial Note

All of *Spectra* is included, along with a selection of the later "Spectric" poems, all of *Cake*, and one third each of *Pins for Wings*, *Guest Book*, and *New Poems 1960*. The section of selected verse includes poems published in books and magazines over a period of almost fifty years as well as a few unpublished poems that have turned up among Witter Bynner's papers.

Contents

INTRODUCTION / xi

Spectra (1916) / 3

Later Spectric Poems: A Selection (1917–1927) / 6 1

Posthumous Poems of Emanuel Morgan (1927) / 8 1

Pins for Wings by Emanuel Morgan (1920) / 8 7

Cake: An Indulgence (1926) / 9 7

Guest Book (1935) / 2 0 5

The Deathless Laughers, The Forgotten Gods:
Selected Verse (1907–1954) / 2 2 9

New Poems (1960) / 2 6 3

Introduction

BY WILLIAM JAY SMITH

I

When Witter Bynner died on June 1, 1968, at the age of eighty-seven, a brief *New York Times* obituary notice called attention to his achievement as a translator of Chinese poetry and as the perpetrator, together with his fellow poet, Arthur Davison Ficke, of *Spectra*, one of the most famous literary hoaxes of the twentieth century. Although Bynner had every right to be remembered for those two things, this did seem rather brief and unfair treatment of one who had several decades before been considered one of the country's leading poets. Between the publication of his first book of poems at the age of twenty-six, *An Ode to Harvard and Other Poems*, in 1907, and his last, *New Poems 1960*, he had brought out many volumes of poetry and plays. With his friend Edna St. Vincent Millay and his rival Amy Lowell, he had been at the center of the new poetry movement in the United States before and after World War I. His poems had appeared for decades in such magazines as *The New Yorker*, *Poetry*, *The Nation*, and *The New Republic*. In more popular newspapers and journals his verse had been read by thousands of appreciative readers, and he had composed a number of lyrics that seemed destined to endure. He had written biography and criticism and, as a teacher, had inspired and encouraged the young. He was one of the first literary figures to espouse fervently the rights of both women and blacks, and during his long residence in Santa Fe he had been a strong supporter of the American Indian. Bynner's achievements as a poet were recognized toward the end of his long career by his election to the position of Chancellor of the Academy of American Poets and to membership in the National Institute (now the American Academy and Institute) of Arts and Letters. Yet at the time of his death he was chiefly remembered for his translations of Chinese poetry and for his part in a hoax. After the successful reception of *Spectra*, which appeared in 1916 as a parody of current literary movements and was taken seriously by critics of the time, Bynner had remarked that he and his friend Ficke had with this spoof created a monster that would get the better of them both. It seemed in a way that it had.

Witter Bynner, as an editor of the publishing house of Small, Maynard and Company, had arranged for Ezra Pound's initial publication in the United States with the three volumes *Provença: Poems Selected from Personae, Exultations, and Canzoniere* (1910), *Sonnets and Ballate of Guido Cavalcanti* (1912), and *Ripostes* (1913). He later described how Pound had come to call on him in New York bringing a sheaf of manuscripts and wearing, although the weather was cool, a broad-brimmed straw hat, the white band of which was decorated with large pink polka dots. "Jacket, vest, and trousers were," Bynner said, "of three colors—mauve, snuff-colored, and purplish—and his socks bright-hued in shoes one black, one blue. He told me that he yearned to go to Europe and that his father, for some reason, wanted advice according to my judgment of the son's manuscripts. I think there was a note to the effect, 'I'll help him if you say so.' And I said so."

Pound was only the first of a number of poets whom Bynner was to encourage. In his autobiography, *The House on Jefferson Street*, Horace Gregory recalls, while a student at the University of Wisconsin in the early twenties, his first encounter with Witter Bynner:

> Then at the height of his own career as a poet, he had heard of some light verse I had written, read it in an undergraduate magazine and praised it, and then, by a grape-vine route, invited me to meet him for tea at the house of a

mutual friend. He was on his way, so I heard, back home from China, his head filled with adventures he had had there—and now he stood before me, a tall, balding man, with the gestures of a Boston mandarin, smiling down at me, holding a steaming hot cup of tea in his right hand. With the grace of an accomplished actor, he dropped, cross-legged, to a cushion at my feet, and looked up at me. He then began spinning a web of small talk, of a kind that seemed to charm everyone around us—and at that moment I thought of him as a citizen of the large world I hoped to enter after leaving the university. At this party, Bynner never seemed the guest, but throughout it, the welcoming and engaging host; even the intonations of his voice flattered everyone there; he had made an art of meeting people, and putting them at their unguarded ease. Years later, when I had read of his friendship with D. H. and Frieda Lawrence in New Mexico, I understood why they found his attentions so flattering.

Many years later when I was myself an undergraduate at Washington University in St. Louis, Witter Bynner was the first nationally known poet to praise one of my poems. Along with Clark Mills and Tennessee (Tom) Williams, I was then a member of the local chapter of the College Poetry Society, which issued regularly—edited from the University of Wyoming by its founder, Ann Winslow—a magazine entitled *College Verse*, to which members in colleges throughout the country contributed. Ann Winslow had edited an anthology, *Trial Balances*, with contributions by older student members and appreciations of them by established poets, a book that helped launch the careers of Theodore Roethke, Elizabeth Bishop, Josephine Miles, and others. With his characteristic generosity (he had earlier set up a college poetry prize through the Poetry Society of America and a high-school prize through *Scholastic* magazine), Witter Bynner served as judge for one of *College Verse*'s annual contests in the late thirties. He chose my poem "He Will Not Hear" as the winner. A few years later when Tennessee Williams left St.

Louis on one of his first trips to the Southwest and the West Coast, he stayed with Bynner in Santa Fe and brought back several of Bynner's books, which he left with me in St. Louis when he departed again. It was not until some fifteen years afterward, however, that I met the man whose words of praise had meant so much to me as a very young writer.

In May 1950, when Barbara Howes and I were living in San Domenico above Florence, we heard from our friend and neighbor, the conductor Newell Jenkins, that Witter Bynner was visiting the city. I invited him and his friend Robert Hunt to dinner. On the loggia of what had once been the peasant house on the estate of Walter Savage Landor, surrounded by the cypresses that Landor himself had planted, we heard for the first time of *Spectra*, a tale of literary complication and intrigue as unbelievable as it was amusing. Bynner punctuated his account of the hoax with the boom, snort, and crackle of his laughter, and he soon had us all laughing as well. At the conclusion of the evening I asked him to put down a few lines from one of his poems in our guestbook. He composed on the spot a couplet, which has the graceful light touch that I had discovered in so much of his work:

> Cypresses, laurels, are what earth intends,
> Into which man intrudes,—and yet with friends.

It was only when he took up the book, brought it next to his eyes, and began to write in his close and careful script that we realized that he was almost blind. We saw him again a number of times in Florence and then, when we went to Venice the following week with Eudora Welty, met him on the Piazza San Marco, where the sharp salvos of his laughter were a fitting accompaniment to the languid pieces the string orchestra was playing in the bright sunlight. He appeared to be enjoying every minute of his visit to that city, the visual delights of which must have reached him in only the most blurred of outlines.

Horace Gregory tells of having seen Bynner for the last

time in 1957 in Athens: "He was deeply tanned, venerable, and bright, for he seemed to have drifted into one of the rare havens of extreme old age. He confessed to me that he was almost blind, but that Greek white light from Apollo overhead and the heat of mid-July had restored his senses—there now, he could see me clearly—the fog had dropped away. The last I saw of him was a wave of a long brown hand." This was the same Bynner whom I saw when I stayed with him for about ten days in Santa Fe—in November 1958—venerable, bright, and extremely gracious. It was only when he himself called attention to it, as he had done with Horace Gregory, that anyone was aware of his almost total blindness. I had been in correspondence with him since our meetings in Italy and, having dined out many times on the story of the *Spectra* hoax, had decided with his help to tell the story in full for the first time. I had come out to Santa Fe to go over with him the material that he had concerning it.

Harold Witter Bynner—or "Hal," as he was known to his friends—was in a particularly jovial mood during my stay, delighted to be reliving with complete clarity of mind the amusing events that had taken place forty years before. I am not myself a "morning person," preferring, if I have the choice, to write after lunch. It was not difficult, therefore, for me to adjust to the routine of the Bynner household. Nobody in the house arose before noon, when Rita Padilla, Bynner's devoted servant of many years, fixed a hearty breakfast. Bynner and I would retire after lunch to his studio to work, and then after dinner friends would come by and talk would continue until two or three in the morning. Bynner's house on the corner of Buena Vista and College Streets in Santa Fe, now the property of St. John's College, was like a series of Chinese boxes spilled out on different levels and separated in some places by courtyards. It was filled with a jumble of American Indian, Mexican, and Chinese artifacts, some of considerable value and others collected for sentimental reasons. The ensemble had a warm and pleasant feeling about it, but the odd mixture had prompted one of

Bynner's old friends, the Santa Fe artist Gustave Baumann, to refer to the house as Hal Bynner's "Chinese Laundry."

The walls of Bynner's studio were covered with signed photographs of writers and artists, many of which he had taken himself, dating back to the beginning of his career. Bynner was born in Brooklyn, New York, in 1881. (His uncle Edwin Lassetter Bynner had been the author of *Agnes Surriage* and other popular novels.) He attended high school in Brookline, Massachusetts, and went on to Harvard, where he was on the staff of *The Harvard Advocate*. After his graduation he became assistant editor of *McClure's* magazine, and a literary adviser of the publishers McClure, Phillips and Company. He lived for a decade at Cornish, New Hampshire, made two trips in 1917 and 1920 to China and the Orient, and, after teaching for a year at the University of California at Berkeley, settled in Santa Fe, where he spent most of the remainder of his life, except for frequent visits to Chapala, Mexico.

All those who had the pleasure of knowing Hal Bynner were struck by his tremendous vitality and love of life. A young visitor, Katharine Van Stone (now Mrs. Walter M. Mayer), came to his house in Santa Fe in the twenties and described him thus: "Hal is a big man, over six feet tall and of corresponding weight. He is about forty years old, and has brown eyes and hair; he always wears eccentric clothes and that night he had on a pair of wide white Mexican trousers, a brilliant purple velvet Navajo shirt, handmade native shoes and a heavy silver belt. His amazing vitality and joy in living every minute to the fullest shone through his face." He had developed this joy of living at Harvard, where he had been a friend of both Wallace Stevens and Franklin Delano Roosevelt, and it never left him. Paul Horgan has described the Harvard that Bynner then knew, when the great professors who have since become legendary—James, Santayana, Kittredge—were all there: "Boston was still the Athens of pre-Hollywood America. College boys believed in pranks, and practised them, hoping for shocks of indrawn breath when discovered. Undergraduates supered in the opera seasons, and once when Bernhardt played Boston, Bynner and friends 'took the horses out of her shafts' and pulled her sleigh crying and chiming through the snow. The actress wore lavish furs dyed pink, and kissed her fabulous hands at the sidewalks, indulging the convention with propriety, murmuring glad little profanities of appreciation through the peony-red mouth in her blanched mask. A running pack of young males was surely the happiest society in the world. How beautiful to believe in the God of democratic love, literature, and the rights of conscious folly!"

It was at Harvard that he developed the gift for mimicry that never left him. It was as a young super at the Boston opera that he witnessed performances of the celebrated Emma Eames. For his friends he frequently did an impersonation of her as the curtain came down on Gounod's *Romeo and Juliet*. The hefty Madame Eames would bow toward the audience with icy correctness, a fixed smile on her face as she moved back majestically and edged over in her statuesque way into the wings and, as soon as she reached there, would turn toward the young supers and stagehands and let out a steady stream of profanity for all that had gone wrong during the performance, and then, without losing her poise for a moment, return to the stage for yet another stately bow.

Bynner developed his dramatic gift until he was an accomplished drawing-room actor—a kind of masculine Ruth Draper—entertaining his friends by the hour and delighting to take the parts of any number of characters. One of his favorite set pieces was an impersonation of his Aunt Louisa in New Hampshire on the occasion of her one hundredth birthday. With a shawl around his head and without his teeth and glasses, he would demonstrate how the wind came through a window that had been left open and hurled Aunt Louisa round and round and finally off over the hillside while she continued to utter her shrill inanities. He told hilarious stories also about his savagely independent, eccentric, and rich mother, Mrs. Walter Wellington, who at one time occupied two apartments in the Hotel Seymour in New York and, distrusting both banks and Franklin Roosevelt, kept a half million dollars in bills in one of her closets. He also impersonated writers he had known over the years—D. H. Lawrence, Henry James, and Theodore Dreiser.

As a very young man Bynner had made a pilgrimage to see George Meredith. He had met Henry James in New York in 1905 and corresponded with him. He arranged for the first publication in the United States of A. E. Housman, whom he greatly admired. As a close friend of Clara Clemens, he had gone often to see her and her father, Mark Twain, in New York. On one such visit he asked Mark Twain what he had been reading. "I don't read," the old man barked, "I write."

During the Santa Fe evenings I had many examples of Witter Bynner's delight in verbal play. He was in his old age a resplendent Rabelaisian character who enjoyed earthy jokes and bawdy limericks, which he composed easily and well. He had through the years been something of a playboy, but his favorite play had always been with words. He took inordinate pleasure in puns, and he was the first to realize that his own name lent itself to no end of them. I had remembered reading somewhere the perhaps apocryphal account of a drunken Hart Crane stumbling up to him once in Mexico and saying icily, "Witter Bynner, you're going to have a bitter winter." (O. Henry, in letters to Bynner, addressed him with many variations on his name, one of which was "Mr. Bitter Winter.") Bynner himself told of having replaced the drama critic William Winter for a lecture in Pittsburgh. Knowing that his audience would not be exactly pleased to hear a young and relatively unknown poet instead of the well-known critic, Bynner announced himself by saying, "I am the *Witter* of your discontent." It was in *Spectra*, the remarkable hoax published in 1916, that Bynner's sense of verbal play and his dramatic and satiric gifts first made themselves known to a wide audience.

II

In February 1916, on the way to visit his Harvard friend and fellow poet, Arthur Davison Ficke, who was then living in Davenport, Iowa, Witter Bynner stopped off at Chicago. While there he attended a performance of the Diaghilev Ballet Russe in the company of Laird Bell and Howard Vincent O'Brien. During the intermission, after a performance of *Le Spectre de la Rose*, danced by Massine, Bynner discussed with his friends the absurdity of some of the recent poetic "schools." There were the Imagists, the Vorticists, and the Futurists, of course, but had they heard, he asked—glancing up from his program with a resounding laugh—of the *Spectrists*, the new poets who had just appeared in Pittsburgh; *they* were the ones to watch. Bynner, who had just come from Pittsburgh and who had been thinking what a good idea it would be to found a new school and to have some "fun with the extremists and with those of the critics who were overanxious to be in the van," found himself, with this chance but inspired conversational gambit, faced with a virtual *fait accompli*. The possibilities of the words "spectral" or "spectric" flashed over him in a moment, and he remembered them when en route to Davenport the following day. He composed the first three poems on the train, and on arriving at Davenport, set forth to Arthur Davison Ficke and his wife his plan for a burlesque. Ficke, who was just as irritated as Bynner by the "schools" of the moment and who also thoroughly enjoyed a good joke, entered immediately into the spirit of the occasion. The Spectrists that evening came into being.

The first problem, before producing more Spectric poems, was to settle on the names of the writers. Names "of a foreign tinge" were wanted "as making the school more impressive to mere Americans." Bynner's choice was, he recalled, "lumberingly poetic—the first part of it being a suggestion of 'I Hear Emmanuel Singing' and the second a sound reflecting the German word *morgen*—so that the rather misty idea was 'morning song.'" He visualized Morgan as a middle-aged gentleman with a long, square-cut beard. Arthur Davison Ficke, remembering having seen in the culinary columns of some Sunday newspaper a recipe for the then little-known Jewish pastries called knishes, decided on "Anne Knish." Aware of the humorous Yiddish-vaudeville sound of the word, although not perhaps of its full Yiddish meaning, he saw Miss—or Mrs. (she was probably divorced)—

Knish as a Hungarian lady who, through wide experiences, had kept an open mind and a pure soul. The personalities of the mythical writers became more clearly outlined in proportion to the "spectra" or "spectrics" produced; and these were written at a fast clip. In fact, the poets became so absorbed in their productions that the constant composition and recitation of Spectric verse was too much for Mrs. Ficke. She ordered the pair out of the house until they had finished their manuscript. They retired to a hotel across the river in Moline, Illinois, where, as Arthur Davison Ficke put it, from ten quarts of excellent Scotch in ten days they extracted the whole of Spectric philosophy.

Little did they realize how soon their creation would descend on the unsuspecting public. They had three copies of the manuscript bound, one each for themselves and one to send to the publisher Mitchell Kennerley, who had published both poets under their own names. Kennerley, to their great astonishment, accepted it at once for publication, apparently (as Bynner remembered it) as a bona fide manuscript; and when informed of the real identity of the authors, agreed to keep the secret.

Not all readers of poetry, however keen their interest, could follow the Spectric adumbrations of Anne Knish's preface to the volume (one reviewer indeed found the preface as "brilliant as a rainy midnight in the country") but there was no doubt that before many months had passed the Spectrists had arrived. At a time when "schools" were springing up everywhere like daisies in a field or crabgrass on a lawn, here was a new group that had rooted out all the rest. The Vorticists, the Imagists, the Futurists, the Chorists now were passé; the Spectrists had moved into the front ranks of the avant-garde. Edgar Lee Masters, in a letter to Emanuel Morgan dated December 1, 1916, wrote that he thought highly of *Spectra*, "an idea capable of great development along creative lines," and that Spectrism was "at the core of things and imagism at the surface." Other poets and critics of note were equally impressed: John Gould Fletcher spoke of the Spectrists' "vividly memorable lines"; William Marion Reedy in *Reedy's Mirror* hailed them in glowing terms. Eunice Tietjens, associate editor of *Poetry*, wrote of *Spectra* to Mr. Morgan on May 9, 1917: "It is a real delight!" Headlines in newspapers throughout the country ushered them in, and soon the word "Spectra" was on every tongue. Not everybody liked this newest of poetry; but then that was to be expected—not everybody likes poetry anyway. Still, the Spectrists were facts, as Don Marquis pointed out in the New York *Evening Sun* of December 26, 1916. "Are you hep to the Spectric Group?" he wrote. "Have you a little Spectrist in Your Home?"

Not everyone had. Although Amy Lowell is said to have enthusiastically recommended the volume to a group of apprentice poets at Harvard, she appeared to be on the whole unimpressed. Certainly as the "fair Trotsky" of the Imagist revolution, as H. L. Mencken termed her, she was scarcely ready to welcome competition, and it is reasonable to assume that she had her doubts. The New York *Herald* of December 29, 1916, referred to Spectric poetry as "daughter of Futurist poetry, a granddaughter of *vers libre*, and no relation at all to real poetry." Quoting Mr. Morgan's *Opus 40*:

> Two cocktails round a smile,
>   A grapefruit after grace,
> Flowers in an aisle
>   . . . Were your face.
>
> A strap in a street-car,
>   A sea-fan on the sand,
> A beer on a bar
>   . . . Were your hand.
>
> The pillar of a porch,
>   The tapering of an egg,
> The pine of a torch
>   . . . Were your leg.—

> Sun on the Hellespont,
>   White swimmers in the bowl
> Of the baptismal font
>   Are your soul.

the Detroit *News Tribune* of January 18, 1917, asked: "Are we justified in saying that the poetic and the very spectric likeness of a hand to a beer has never before been revealed to the public? And almost anyone would love to have a leg like a porch support."

But whatever doubts were raised and whatever hesitations expressed, Mr. Morgan's humor and Miss Knish's tangle of sense imagery had made their point and were to gain more and more adherents during the course of the next year and a half. Letters poured into Pittsburgh requesting the advice and opinion of Morgan and Knish on a variety of subjects; little magazines asked for the latest Spectric products. Harriet Monroe accepted several new poems of Emanuel Morgan for publication in *Poetry*, thereby giving him the seal of approval of the official organ of the American poetic renaissance. *Reedy's Mirror*, which had welcomed Spectrism from the start, also opened its pages to Mr. Morgan; *The Little Review* had its readers illuminated by the latest rays from the spectrum with the publication in its issue of July 1917 of Mr. Morgan's *Opus 96*. One of the most influential and advanced of the little magazines was *Others*, edited from New York by Alfred Kreymborg and backed by Walter Conrad Arensberg, one of the first great patrons of modern art. As the successor of the *Glebe*, it had sponsored the first appearance in February 1914, in successive issues, of "Peter Quince at the Clavier" by Wallace Stevens and "Portrait of a Lady" by T. S. Eliot. *Others*, whose motto was "The old expressions are with us always and there are always others," had brought out a special issue in October 1915 of dance poems of the Choric School. It was only natural then that it should devote a special issue in January 1917 to the Spectric School: the Spectric poems might not involve the dance, but they were certainly filled with action and with "other" expressions. The Spectric *Others* opened with *Opus 344* of Anne Knish, the opus number apparently indicating the extent of Miss Knish's feverish poetic activity since her original publication.

The two poets decided on Pittsburgh as the home of Mr. Morgan and Miss Knish because they believed that there would be less danger of the secret being ferreted out there, "since interest in schools of poetry is not the big thing in the life of the average Pittsburgher." "But we had to do something," Bynner recalled at that period, "about the letters that came to the poets, so we gave as Emanuel Morgan's address, the address of a lady in Pittsburgh whom I know—a lady who hates everything that savors of Vorticism or Imagism!—and she, poor thing, was promptly deluged with letters about Spectrism."

The Pittsburgh poets had no difficulty making their own way in the world, but Bynner and Ficke soon found that they had ample opportunity to help the mythical Morgan and Knish establish themselves in the literary firmament. In the summer of 1916, before the book's publication, Herbert Croly, the founder of *The New Republic,* and Philip Littell, its literary editor, were dining in Cornish, New Hampshire, at the house of Homer Saint-Gaudens, where Bynner was then living. When the two men noticed the proofs of *Spectra* lying on his worktable, Bynner feared that the end had come. He recovered himself in time to say, however, that this was an advance copy of a book sent to him for comment and that the publisher evidently had great confidence in it. Both Croly and Littell, delighted to have happened on something so new and vigorous as *Spectra,* urged Bynner to review the volume for *The New Republic.* Naturally he took pleasure in complying with the request, and even greater pleasure in collecting the fifteen dollars he was paid for his article.

With the deadline for the Spectric issue of *Others* only a few days off, the two poets, having failed in their search for disciples, found themselves together again at Davenport, Iowa; and they retired once more across the river to Moline, Illinois, this time to the home of Marjorie Allen Seiffert, a well-known poet of the Chicago school. Harriet Monroe in her autobiography remembers Mrs. Seiffert as a "round-faced, red-cheeked beauty," who belonged to "a supersophisticated little 'smart set' group" in the tri-cities of Moline, Rock Island, and Davenport, people whose grandfathers had made their fortunes in the manufacture of "the first steel plows and other agricultural aids." "Their dinners were superlative for food and service," wrote Miss Monroe, "and for a quick fencing of witty talk among intimates intellectually up to date." When at such a dinner the perpetrators of the hoax explained their predicament to Mrs. Seiffert, she tried immediately and failed, as the others had, and the gentlemen then resorted to force "part jolly, part desperate." "We had told our tale to her in her bedroom, where she was making further efforts to be Spectric," Bynner remembered later, "and into it we locked her, determined that not until she had become Spectric should she emerge." While the party downstairs enjoyed cocktails and part of dinner, Mrs. Seiffert labored "almost angrily" until from a succession of manuscripts that she thrust under the door Witter Bynner and Arthur Ficke selected a number they considered worthy of inclusion. She chose the name Elijah Hay almost as soon as she was released from her imprisonment, and the verses she had written appeared with scarcely any change in the Spectric *Others.*

With a cousin acting as scribe and go-between, Mrs. Seiffert —as Mr. Hay—carried on a correspondence over a period of months with Dr. William Carlos Williams, Alfred Kreymborg, and others. When Dr. Williams wrote saying that he preferred Morgan and Hay to Knish because she took the whole matter too seriously, Mrs. Seiffert forwarded the letter to Witter Bynner with the comment: "The cream of the whole thing is that Arthur, who especially scorns the whole business, is criticized as taking it too seriously! And what a wonderful argument for the feminist cause that we poor women cannot take our verses in a lighter vein!"

As the cause gained ground, the Spectrists often had the

pleasure of being presented to themselves. Alfred Kreymborg, announcing personally to Witter Bynner that he had persuaded the Spectrists to compile an issue of *Others*, assured him that the school was genuine since friends of his were acquainted with both the founders, and that Anne Knish was, of course, a devastating beauty. Indeed, the hoax might well have continued months longer had it not been for America's entry into World War I. It soon became difficult to joke about anything, even about the state of American letters.

Arthur Ficke's Spectric monster, undismayed by the Atlantic, followed him to France and surprised him there in what constitutes one of the truly surrealistic consequences of the hoax. Ficke, a judge advocate wearing the uniform of a United States Army captain and "trembling with awe," breakfasted one morning in Paris with a brigadier general of the regular army, whom he had known slightly during peacetime. Their conversation turned to literary matters and the general brought up the subject of *Spectra*. He asked Ficke if he supposed the book to be genuine or just a hoax. Arthur Ficke answered that, although many people whose opinions he respected took the volume seriously, he himself had always been inclined to suspect that it was fake. The general congratulated him smilingly on his astuteness, and said firmly that he was quite right. Asked how he could be so sure, the general replied all the more firmly, "Because I myself am Anne Knish." Naturally Ficke then plied him with questions about the whole affair and begged him to reveal the identity of Emanuel Morgan, but the general declared that he was under oath not to do so. Arthur Ficke understandably described this encounter as one of "the most deliriously happy hours I have ever spent."

In autumn of 1917 word had begun to get around in the literary world that the Spectrists might not be all they seemed. Mrs. Seiffert contended that suspicion had naturally attached itself to Witter Bynner because he was "so crazy about the delightful myth" that he would "introduce *Spectra* into the most unlikely conversations." In an address before the Fortnightly

Club at Chicago in May 1916, he said: "Most of this schismatic poetry is nothing but rot. How one can take up his time with it is beyond me." Bynner did, however, see a ray of hope in the Spectrists, samples of whose work, he said, had reached him before publication. Quoting Emanuel Morgan's *Opus 62*, which begins:

> Three little creatures gloomed across the floor
>   And stood profound in front of me,
>   And one was Faith, and one was Hope,
>   And one was Charity.

he went on: "Now of course this sort of stuff isn't quite so hopeless as some of the other, but what does it mean? A few may see intelligence in it." Bynner was asking similar questions about the Spectrists nearly two years later on April 19, 1918, during a speech before the Twentieth Century Club in Detroit. He was challenged midway in his lecture, to his utter amazement, by a young man who asked simply and directly, "Is it not true, Mr. Bynner, that you are Emanuel Morgan and that Arthur Davison Ficke is Anne Knish?" Bynner's answer was just as straightforward: it was "Yes." (The challenger had probably come from the University of Wisconsin, where the editors of the *Wisconsin Literary Magazine,* parodying a parody, had presented the work of Manual Organ and Nanne Pish of the Ultra-Violet School of Poetry in their January 1917 issue.)

Newspaper columns across the country dealt even more fully with *Spectra* once the true identities of the writers had been revealed. *The New York Times* took pride in announcing, in a summary of the hoax, that it had not reviewed the book in the first place. The *St. Louis Post-Dispatch* had said of the original publication that "for those who like this sort of thing this is the sort of thing they like," thereby quoting without realizing it a remark that originated with Max Beerbohm and that was later attributed to the Greeks, a miniature hoax in itself. It now called the book one in which there was neither rhyme nor reason. Many of the magazine editors who had warmly welcomed

Spectra were now noticeably silent. Harriet Monroe, who had accepted five poems of Emanuel Morgan's and one of Elijah Hay's for publication in *Poetry*, refused to print them. Jane Heap of *The Little Review*, which had published *Opus 96* by Emanuel Morgan in its July 1918 number, quoted a letter Ezra Pound had written on August 10, 1917, in which he said, "Morgan's 'spectric' business is a little late. People intending to be 'schools' should have 'done it first.' . . . Morgan is only another Imagist imitator with a different preface from Amy's."

Amy Lowell was clearly relieved that the New Poetry, in her eyes the "most national" thing that America had to offer, along with skyscrapers and ice water, was still hers to command: Ezra Pound she had already dismissed and there was *no* Emanuel Morgan. While she continued a friendly correspondence for some time with Witter Bynner, she never really forgave him; he became her official enemy.

William Carlos Williams, recalling the episode years later, wrote to me, "As far as I remember I was completely taken in by the hoax and while not subscribing in every case to the excellence of the poems admired them as a whole quite sincerely." Alfred Kreymborg maintained—and he repeated the judgment later in his critical work *Our Singing Strength*—that the Spectrist poems of Emanuel Morgan and Anne Knish were superior to anything that Bynner and Ficke had published under their own names.

The two poets were ready to admit that, to some extent, the joke was on them. Shortly after the disclosure, Witter Bynner commented sadly that he could not get rid of Emanuel Morgan. "I find now that I write like him without the slightest effort— I don't know where he leaves off and I begin. He's a boomerang!"

Naturally much of *Spectra*, with its intimations of free love and drunkenness, its suggestions of French heels, bobbed hair, the noise of trolley cars, and the dance of Isadora Duncan, its use of words like "cocktail," "cigarette," and "sin," appears far less daring now than it did in its own time. And yet it holds our attention not only because it recalls an interesting period but also because it satirizes certain poetic poses that are still very much with us. Its influence was perhaps more beneficial than one would at first suppose—on both the readers and the critics of poetry and on Witter Bynner himself.

III

The career of Emanuel Morgan did not end with the exposure of the hoax. Although he published *The Beloved Stranger* (as *Songs of the Unknown Lover*) in *Reedy's Mirror* in 1918, and later in book form in 1919 under his own name, Witter Bynner wrote it "as Emanuel Morgan." It was ironic that the preface to this volume was written by William Marion Reedy, one of the first to express enthusiasm for Morgan.

In one poem, "Self-Portrait," omitted from the published sequence of *The Beloved Stranger* but quoted by Reedy in his preface, Emanuel Morgan, as Witter Bynner's *Doppelgänger*, is revealed in a kind of shadowy and humorous self-denial:

> I saw myself sitting at the next table,
> But only in profile;
> The mettle of color was there
> On the cheekbone,
> And the little crepe moustache
> Though not black enough,
> And the lower lip
> Drooping like a rope in water,
> And the nose curving to ruin like the Chinese wall
> With its little dark gates of old life . . .
>
> But when the full face turned,
> I knew again
> That there was no such person.

While this portrait was too frivolous for final inclusion in *The Beloved Stranger*, the book is not without humor, and its middle section, "A Divertisement for the Unknown Lover," placed between "Two Books of Song," has much of the forthright zaniness of *Spectra*. Each fragment of "A Divertisement" reflects the lover's rapidly changing reactions and is introduced by an active verb all the way from "I Change" through "I Kill," "I Accuse," to "I Vanish." Some of the lines such as those of "I Evade," which Bynner appears originally to have intended to publish in *Spectra* or elsewhere as the work of Emanuel Morgan, found their proper place here:

> The look in your eyes
> Was as soft as the underside of soap in a soap-dish . . .
>
> And I left before you could love me.

Louis V. Ledoux, a young poet who later became a well-known collector of Oriental artifacts, wrote to Emanuel Morgan on receiving a copy of *Spectra:* "Some of the poems, quite naturally, appeal to me more than others do, but in most of them is that curious Oriental quality that interested me especially because that particular Orientalism is unusual in our literature." The Oriental quality of *Spectra* was, of course, entirely superficial and was in reality a kind of verbal chinoiserie meant to parody the Imagists, as in the lines:

> I think I must have been born in such a forest,
> Or in the tangle of a Chinese screen.

or:

> Tax-assessors frequently overlook valuables.
> Today they noted my jade.
> But my memory of you escaped them.

The Eastern journey Bynner and Ficke took in *Spectra* was a frivolous and imaginary one. After the appearance of the volume, Bynner did, however, actually travel to China, and the influence of Chinese art and poetry, freshly felt in *The Beloved Stranger*, was important and enduring.

In 1954, writing to George N. Kates in admiration of his book *The Years That Were Fat*, Bynner recalled his own first "fat" years in China in 1917 and 1920: "Seoul, Mukden, Peking, Nanking, Chinkiang, Shanghai, Hangchow, Mokanshan, the coast cities southward to Canton, then being stripped by modernity of its carved and gilded shop-fronts, heaps of them being burned in the streets and the walls torn down for trolley-cars, the abbot's guest on Silver Island, the Yangtse voyage to Chungking, an adventure in those days, then down to Changsha, all this latter part through warring country! How different from your fine rootage in Peking!—and yet not, for I was much of the time travelling with Chinese friends and was often in Chinese dress, partly to be bothered less by Chinese curiosity, which was never really obnoxious but constant. And the great calm of China, in the midst of the travel and the noise. On my last night, though I was due at a supper with Mischa Elman, I ate alone in my room at a Shanghai native hotel, a banquet of all my favorite dishes, taking a little of each and, being vulgarer than you, in tears."

So many American and British poets have in the past fifty years composed imitations of varying degrees of merit of Chinese and Japanese poetry that it is well to remember that Bynner was among the first to make the Chinese manner his own. The poems of *The Beloved Stranger* are not imitations, William Marion Reedy says in his preface, "but absorptions of the Eastern spirit, that spirit compelling the manner." The poet proceeds throughout by indirection, touching with deft brush strokes and with unusually vivid sensuous detail on his experience and allowing the reader to complete the whole. The actual Japanese verse forms of *haiku* and *tanka* are not copied exactly but suggested, as in "Horses":

> Words are hoops
> Through which to leap upon meanings,
> Which are horses' backs,
> Bare, moving.

or "The Fire-mountain":

> Forget you?—
> Can that Hawaiian volcano
> Forget its quick fountains and cascades
> Of fire?

An atmosphere of disembodiment and timelessness is communicated throughout the sequence in poems such as "The Boatmen":

> A nearing benison of boatmen singing . . .
> Can they be bringing to me a new wonder?
>
> They are waiting in the night, as for a passenger . . .
> But who would embark now with no light at all?
>
> The dark is shaking like a tambourine . . .
> They are taking my old wonder.

For all the sensuous detail that the poems contain, the lover is always ethereal and never fully delineated physically; indeed, the being who is addressed seems peculiarly androgynous. The earth itself is sexless, as in "The Canyon":

> It is the dead sex of the earth
> On which the sun still gazes.
>
> It is all the mountains of love,
> Into whose sarcophagus
> Peers
> The moon.

The poems are brief musical notations of feeling, projections of what Jung calls the *anima*. The beloved stranger is "the wandering spirit of the most beloved place." The poet asks:

> For how could the motion of a shadow in a field
> Be a person?

The poems read like the Lucy poems of Wordsworth presented in a light and witty Post-Impressionist manner by a poet with a Buddhist rather than a Christian orientation. Indeed, the sole Christian reference comes toward the end of the book with the word "crucified":

> When I am crucified upon this brow,
> Will the strange god be at peace?

This reference was taken literally by Bynner's friend Paul Thévenaz, whose drawing for the dust jacket shows a crucified Christ superimposed on the face of a Buddha, an image that misses the work's Oriental delicacy and serious playfulness.

•

In *The Beloved Stranger* Bynner's light touch is triumphant, and the scale is never tipped too greatly toward frivolity or triviality. The same cannot be said for all of *Pins for Wings*, which appeared under the name of Emanuel Morgan in 1920. Here the "spectra" of many of Morgan's contemporaries are recorded with true "spectric" accuracy; many of the "pins," which hold the wings to the board, seem sparklingly pointed:

Gertrude Stein

> wings rotting
> under water

Gabriele D'Annunzio

> a passion-flower
> dipped in ammonia

Robinson Jeffers

Aimee Semple McPherson
in a thunderstorm

H.D.

the Winged Victory
hopping

Some of the epithets sound like fragments of conversation from a Firbank novel:

Sarah N. Cleghorn

the rosy half
of an old apple

John Gould Fletcher

two halves of a typewriter
still moving

John Erskine

marbles
in a muff

One of Firbank's ladies exclaims to her companion in utter exasperation, "I should like to *shake* Switzerland." In the best of the *Pins* the mighty like the Alps are indeed shaken and pinned to the wall, but the book is much too long and some of the pins are about as pointed as wads of gum. Emanuel Morgan and Anne Knish are both aptly characterized:

Emanuel Morgan

a bat
and a butterfly
mating

Anne Knish

> a gargoyle
> remembering

but Witter Bynner himself becomes rather lamely:

> God
> in the sugar-bowl

Sending his friend Haniel Long several pages of manuscript of *Pins for Wings* on September 6, 1918, Bynner wrote: "All but three of these were written two years ago. They didn't seem to be W.B.'s. I've fished them out of the notebook, and find them E.M.'s. He *won't* die!" I have before me, as I write, a page of that notebook which Witter Bynner gave me. It looks as if it had been written by a bat or a butterfly on the wing; the script is so small that it can be made out in places only with a magnifying glass. The best of the final *Pins* appear, as indeed they should, to have been tossed off quickly, but in reality, judging by my notebook page and by the manuscript copy sent to Haniel Long, most of them were heavily worked over. *Conrad Aiken*, for example, was first put down as:

> a lightning-conductor
> of suppressed desires
> in Cambridge

Haniel Long commented in the margin: "Cutting! Is it advisable?" The entry was changed to:

> phosphorescence
> in a mill-wheel

and subsequently, simply and advisedly, to:

> phosphorescent
> plumbing

It was natural that Bynner's dramatic gift should lead him to write for the theater. His early efforts include a one-act play written in collaboration with Cecil B. De Mille. His one-act verse plays, *Tiger* (1913) and *The Little King* (1914), together with his version of *Iphigenia in Tauris* (1915), were issued with two other short plays in *A Book of Plays* (1922), but it was not until his verse comedy *Cake* (1926) that his dramatic talent found full and proper expression.

Of the play Bynner wrote in his *Journey with Genius:* "In 1926 I had published a play called *Cake*, some aspects of which were said to be a satire on Mabel Luhan. The slant was sportive but not, I thought, malicious and, since I had visited several times at her house in Taos, I inscribed a copy I sent her: 'Cast your bread upon Witter and it shall return to you as Cake.' I have heard that she was not amused."

Cake may have been inspired by Mabel Dodge Luhan's poem "Ballad of a Bad Girl," which had been illustrated by D. H. Lawrence and published in the May 1924 issue of *Laughing Horse*, the magazine edited by Witter Bynner's secretary and friend, "Spud" Johnson. The heroine of the poem, suffering from rejection by her mother, straddles her father's walking stick and flies off to heaven in search of God. She makes her way through space, feasting on honey cake and ether. When finally she is about to place her hand upon God's breast, out of it springs a man "with blue, blue eyes and a red, red crest" (D. H. Lawrence). Angrily informing her that there is no place for women in heaven, he kicks her out. Saved by falling into a pansy bed, she places the walking stick back in the hall.

As leader of the cultural scene in Taos, Mabel Dodge Luhan had long resented Witter Bynner's position in Santa Fe. They were like the heads of adjoining principalities, enjoying a polite but spirited rivalry. Mrs. Luhan was convinced that Bynner had been responsible for attracting the growing homosexual colony in Santa Fe. She had given "Spud" Johnson a position as her secretary while he was still under contract to Bynner, and this action, together with the absurd "bad girl" poem, may have been enough to set Bynner off.

Lawrence said that he had read *Cake* with a good deal of amusement: "It is often very witty, and in parts really funny . . . Its fault is perhaps in scattering the scenes over the earth, so destroying some of the unity, maybe. But it remains very amusing—and at last just spiteful, which of course tickles me . . . It's not particularly 'Mabel'—rather a type than a specific person."

In the prologue of *Cake* the Unicorn, "a suave and portly Chamberlain," appears before the curtain carrying his horn "as a staff of office." (There is the obvious irony that a unicorn can be captured only by a pure virgin, whereas this particular mistress has had seven husbands, and there is also a play on the sound of the words *unicorn* and *eunuch-horn*.) He sets the tone of the comedy by explaining that the first scene, which the author had written just to allow people to come in late, has been cut:

> I therefore beg you to imagine, friends,
> A sort of drawing-room, with coal-black drapes
> And drooping lights covered with purple grapes.
> The Lady the play's about is giving a tea,
> Assisted by her Chamberlain, that's me.
> The Lady herself is sitting in the middle,
> And they're listening to a fellow with a fiddle.
> Then everybody talks and no one hears,
> And the Lady sits in the middle, bored to tears.
> That was the scene. It wasn't very much,
> Except that it was done with a modern touch,
> You know the sort of thing, nobody there,
> Each of the guests was just an empty chair,
> And we had the members of the orchestra play
> Things that the empty chairs were supposed to say.

The purple grapes covering the drooping lights and the coal-black drapes suggest something straight out of the Art Deco exhibit that had been held the previous year in Paris, but the conversing chairs anticipate Ionesco by several decades. Bynner like Ionesco shows an uninhibited interest in farcical situations, and, indeed, the play reads like an amalgam of Noël Coward, Cole Porter, and Ionesco, with echoes of Oscar Wilde.

Written largely in deftly handled heroic couplets, Bynner's play has an eighteenth-century flavor, an *opera buffa* elegance that overlies the zaniness of the twenties. The Lady reveals her ennui in her opening speech:

> The trouble with me is I'm bored with being bored.
> How long this living takes! How long, O Lord!
> I have had seven husbands—and that's enough, I think.
> I have come through mysticism, free love, and drink.
> I am offered everything money can buy,
> And yet there's nothing I want—not even to die.

On the advice of a puny psychiatrist, who has cured his own neurosis by watching a Mary Pickford movie nightly, she sets out on a world tour to buy experience. She goes first to heaven (Paris), which turns out to be hell; then to China, Africa, and India. Aching at her core "from excess of cake," she tries everything everywhere only to return in the end to marry her own reluctant Cake-servant, after her Unicorn-chamberlain departs, taking a taxi to Grand Central Station ("Out on the side-walk, blowing his own horn").

The Lady's insatiable sexual appetite becomes an overpowering drive to possess and control all that she touches: wearing a coronet of golden eagles, she is the American bitch goddess who seeks to control the world. The Chinese Mandarin in Act II, asked if he is familiar with her American customs, replies:

> You load your missionaries in your guns,
> And in your motor-cars you breed your sons.
> And now your sons are teaching mine
> That the sign of the cross is a dollar sign.

Monetary symbolism parallels sexual symbolism throughout the play: the chairs on which the Unicorn and the Cake-servant sit beside the Lady's throne are supported by "dollar-signs couchants." At the end of the play it is a toss of the coin that decides that the Lady will marry her Cake-servant. The force of the play is not so much in the portrayal of woman as a savagely destructive, castrating force as it is in its attack on the empty money-mad society for which she speaks.

Cake is double-edged, however, and while it attacks materialistic America, it is at the same time basically a modern morality play, the theme of which is death. The Lady, expecting fornication when she steps into a coffin with the Mandarin, is served a cocktail, a libation symbolizing death. And then when, avid for the "smell of moony blood," she is transported to Africa, her Chamberlain declares:

> I shall find you a jungle haunted
> With obscene birds,
> With reptiles to lash you and with black ooze
> To embrace you the way you choose!
> You shall give your breath
> To a constrictor! And when you are dead,
> A vulture will come with a thin varicose head!

The Unicorn continues despite her protests that she wants a "strong-smelling, black-bodied panther, / Not a foul-smelling, bald-headed bird!"

> If I might only see the hoofs of a wild horse
> Trampling your face and hear your cries
> And watch the vulture plucking out your eyes
> And laugh at your silly hands trying to hold back your
>   bowels
> From a jackal's jowls.

He has his wish fulfilled in the next act when the Lady in India sits on an anthill and, about to faint, falls into the arms of the

Introduction · xxxix

Swami's disciple. He tears out her hair and (with the stage direction indicating *music from Salome, that accompanies the beheading of John the Baptist*) the Lady is revealed on the Height, lying in bed and wearing an enormous multicolored wig. In the final scene the Lady is literally a death's-head. Revived by monkey glands and by yeast cakes brought in a funeral rig, she rises like a grotesque and skeletal Venus from the foam. (Baudelaire's line: "Le sourire éternel de tes trente-deux dents" here comes to mind.) When the Lady exclaims:

> Only a woman like me could have known from the first
> That to yield to the senses is to be accursed.

the lines take on a bitter ironic edge, since she is now deprived of her senses and has come finally home (i.e., to the grave). She has become a ghost; her servants leave her, except for her Cake-servant, who welcomes her invisible guests to empty chairs that are brought onstage to jazz accompaniment:

> The guests! Miss Hare, Mrs. Bacon. Mr. Fox. Mr. Wolf.
>   Miss Catt.
> Dr. Stork and both the Lyons. You can sit down where
>   you're at.

All the devouring beasts of the earthly kingdom are there to greet the Lady as she, wedding her reluctant Cake-servant, enters the Kingdom of Death.

It may be a mistake to claim too much for the symbolism of *Cake*, which so clearly makes fun of itself, but the play has a remarkably resonant depth that may be lost sight of because of its brilliant surface.

Sweeney Agonistes by T. S. Eliot appeared first in *The New Criterion* of October 1926 (as "Fragments of a Prologue") and in January 1927 (as "Fragment of an Agon"), both under the general title *Wanna Go Home, Baby?* There are striking similarities between what Eliot later subtitled "Fragments of an Aristophanic Melodrama" and Bynner's *Cake*, which was completed in June 1926 and published in the fall of that year. In both, the action is stylized as in Noh drama and the characters are caricatures, bent on having a "good time." Both make use of vaudeville routines and catch in their dialogue the syncopated beat of jazz. When in "Sweeney Agonistes" Sweeney wants to carry Doris off to a cannibal—and later a "crocodile"—isle, where there are only three things, "Birth, and copulation, and death," Doris protests:

> DORIS: That's not life, that's no life
> Why I'd just as soon be dead.
>
> SWEENEY: That's what life is. Just is
>
> DORIS: What is?
> What's that life is?
>
> SWEENEY: Life is death.

The Lady in *Cake*, at the other end of the social scale from Doris, is reminded by the Swami when her clothes and food have been removed:

> Nothing is anyone's but solitude—
> And death.

Home, toward which the women in both instances are headed, is, of course, the grave. Eliot's overall intention in stressing Sweeney's discovery of necessity and retribution ("somebody's gotta pay the rent") is naturally different from Bynner's, but many of the elements of the two plays are the same.

When Eliot wrote *The Cocktail Party* twenty years after *Sweeney Agonistes*, he drew on his earlier play and may also have had a look at *Cake*. *The Cocktail Party* opens with an inane cocktail conversation in which Celia asks Julia to tell the story "about Lady Klootz and the wedding cake." The story about Lady Klootz, who according to Julia, "had too much vitality," never gets told, but "cake" and "gin" become the key words in the first scene. Food and drink take on symbolic significance in both plays: in *The Cocktail Party* there is the mess concocted for Edward in the kitchen using up all the eggs, and in *Cake* all the references to cake with their many obvious implications. In both plays, cocktail libations are offered up at the turning point of the action. Both plays mock the modern fetish of psychiatry. Sir Henry Harcourt-Reilly, the psychiatrist, admonishes the characters in *The Cocktail Party* in the words of the dying Buddha to his disciples: "Work out your salvation with diligence"; and the Mandarin in *Cake* (the Oriental doctor), invoking Laotzu, advises the Lady: "Lean with the wind. Accept the universe." Both plays make pointed use of the black humor of cannibalism, and I dare say that *Cake* and *The Cocktail Party* are the only two modern verse dramas—or dramas of any sort for that matter—in which a society woman meets her death in a remote place beside an anthill. I do not wish to belabor the possibility that *Cake* is yet another source for *The Cocktail Party* (the plays are totally different in tone), but only to suggest that *Cake* is a highly entertaining and original comedy that deserves far more attention than it has received.

In *Journey with Genius* Bynner tells the following story about *Cake:* "I had finished the manuscript, placed a stone over it, left it on the ground, and was stretching muscles by making a bonfire nearby of strayed newspapers and waste. A neighbor's little boy had, perhaps justly, thought my pile of scribbled sheets rubbish too, so that by the time I came back with my own next armful the whole manuscript was consumed." Whether this is entirely true is hard to tell since there are other versions of the scene, one by "Spud" Johnson, who has Bynner and a guest chasing tumbleweed rather than newspaper over a hill. In any case, the play was soon rewritten and produced first in June 1927 and then revived late in January 1928 by the Pasadena Community Players under the direction of Gilmor Brown, with a constructivist set designed by Margaret Linley, who had worked with Max Reinhardt. The production was taken to San Francisco, where it received excellent notices. Witter Bynner had written the play with Mrs. Fiske in mind to play the role of the Lady, but the only East Coast production was that of the Harvard Dramatic Club in 1930.

It was some thirty years after the first production of the play when Witter Bynner took me to call on Mabel Dodge Luhan in her house in Taos. It was a November day when a bonfire of tumbleweed and newspaper of the sort that supposedly consumed the manuscript might have been welcome. We passed an Indian at the side of the house—I think it was Tony Luhan—who stared at us and nodded as we went in. Mrs. Luhan had left word that she was ill and could see Bynner only by himself. As I sat in the dark hallway conscious of the ghosts of the Lawrences and others that must be lurking there in the darkness (we had seen that morning in Taos an exhibit of some erotic paintings by D. H. Lawrence), the low drone of the bedroom conversation was broken from time to time by Bynner's explosive laughter. Whatever differences had existed between him and Mrs. Luhan seemed to have been made up long ago. The nearly blind old poet could then barely see the ailing and once-powerful woman who had apparently served so long ago to set in motion his lively satire.

•

The next work that displays Witter Bynner's satirical gifts, *Guest Book* (1935), was ten years in the making. The book consists of a sequence of seventy sonnets portraying people who had supposedly been the poet's guests. In an early draft of *Pins for Wings,* the entry on Edgar Lee Masters reads:

> though he slice a novel
> into tidbits called poems
> can he deceive
> the public?

In *Guest Book* Bynner seems in the same way to be slicing a novel into poetic tidbits, and his publishers on the dust jacket called the book "a sophisticated modern *Spoon River Anthology*."

Guest Book gives us a number of literary portraits. Amy Lowell is again savagely presented as "Poetess":

> She was as callous in the execution
> Of verse as though of Sacco and Vanzetti.
> She knew the academic convolution
> Which gives immense importance to the petty.

Max Eastman is here as "Communist":

> He deems the Russian people half-divine
> Because they happen to live far from here . . .

Robinson Jeffers is drawn as "Jeremiah":

> A ship alive becomes to him a hull
> Charred and undone, the fumble of a wreck;
> His dreams are but the droppings of a gull
> Caught in a noose of seaweed round his neck;
> And crying like a maniac toward the sky,
> He pulls mankind in after him, to die.

Carl Van Vechten is the "Stylist":

> His paunch and visage both assumed a look
> Not national but international
> In spite of all the purgatives he took;
> And while his titles gathered on the shelf,
> The man became fictitious to himself.

And Mabel Dodge Luhan appears again, as in *Cake*, insatiable, as "Gourmande":

> Though she is fed and surfeited and fat,
> She does her best to drink a waterfall—
> Not that she wants the water for a minute,
> But she thinks she had better be round it than be in it.

Much of the book may be read as a trenchant *roman à clef* in verse, and it is understandable that Thornton Wilder, while admiring the psychological insights reflected in many of the portraits, at first advised Bynner against publishing it.

Bynner originally thought of calling the book *Rogue's Gallery*. Some of the best portraits are those of eccentric figures who turned up in Santa Fe from both the East and the West Coasts—and there were apparently many of them during the twenties and thirties. The two sonnets of "Expatriates" present not only incisive portraits of a candy manufacturer's son and his titled English wife but also create, in the manner of Scott Fitzgerald, an entire scene of twenties' decadence. Bynner is precise in pinpointing emptiness and pretension in "Debutante" and "Dowager." Other poems, such as "Dorian," written in couplets, catch with Restoration flavor the macabre essence that lies close beneath a glittering surface:

> He assumes the Morris chair, for Dorian
> Forgets that comfort was Victorian.
> Upholstered in his ease, he puffs the smoke
> Of a jaded super-futuristic joke. . . .
> He gives away his underclothes and hats
> And ties his throat to a fig-tree with cravats.

D. H. Lawrence, who was genuinely fond of Bynner, disliked the democratic side that showed up in the Whitmanian stance of some of his verses. It was this dislike that led Lawrence to picture Bynner as Owen Rhys, the poet in *The Plumed Serpent*, who, suffering from "an American despair of having lived in vain," rushes about trying to take in everything. It is perhaps this aspect that leads Bynner in *Guest Book* to cast his

Introduction · xlv

net too wide and at times to write trivially of trivial people. Often it is sympathy that betrays him: he gets too close to his subject and likes him or her too much to remain objective; the language softens and the toughness edges into sentimentality. It is these lapses in the book that caused some critics to find the irony too genial and the poems lacking in bite.

Bynner in the "Apology" that opens *Guest Book* states that he wishes to show neither malice nor kindness toward his subjects but to present them honestly in their essences, and that if they have faults, their faults are also his. His reader is unconvinced: while he may have wished to give a record of his guests according to the Jonsonian humors, his intent for most of the sequence is clearly satire, the exposure of wickedness and folly. Had he been as ruthless in the execution of verse as he accuses the "Poetess" (Amy Lowell) of being, he would have cut the volume by two thirds. It would then read as unrelenting satire that has something of the poetic insight of Browning and at the same time a Byronic panache.

IV

In the past, light verse meant *vers de société* of the sort written by Voiture at the French court and by the Cavalier poets of England in the seventeenth century. It went from the satirical heroic couplets of the eighteenth century to the frivolities of Austin Dobson in the nineteenth. All of it was characterized by elegance and polish and was the work of an élite or privileged class. W. H. Auden, one of the finest modern writers of light verse, takes a much wider view of it, however, in his introduction to *The Oxford Book of Light Verse* (1938). In his anthology he includes three categories of poetry: "(1) Poetry written for performance, to be spoken or sung before an audience, e.g. Folk-songs, the poems of Tom Moore. (2) Poetry intended to be read, but having for its subject-matter the everyday social life of its period or the experiences of the poet as an ordinary human being, e.g. the poems of Chaucer, Pope, Byron. (3) Such nonsense poetry, as through its properties and technique, has a general appeal (Nursery Rhymes, the poems of Edward Lear)." Light verse, he insists, can be serious: "It has only come to mean *vers de société*, triolets, smoke-room limericks, because, under the social conditions which produced the Romantic Revival, and which have persisted, more or less, ever since, it has been only in trivial matters that poets have felt in sufficient intimacy with their audience to be able to forget themselves and their singing robes."

In the trivial matter of *Spectra* Witter Bynner felt an intimacy with his audience; he found it invigorating to discover that there was a cultivated group, larger than might have been expected, who could join him in laughing down the pomposity and pretension of the poetry of the time. This feeling of intimacy carried over into later serious works. By consciously cultivating over a long period the ancient Chinese manner that makes of lightness a positive virtue, he was able in his best poems to put aside his singing robes and write poems of great delicacy that are at the same time extremely serious. For Bynner to put aside those robes, however, was not always easy. Edgar Lee Masters, in his introduction to the revision of *Grenstone Poems* (1926), said of Bynner's books: "They have appealed to me because they arise out of a democratic feeling, and an inclusive sympathy which takes in all humanity." It is this democratic feeling and inclusive sympathy that caused Bynner over the years to write some of his least successful poems. Democratic feeling was certainly behind "The Thunder-Bringer," written in 1916, which contains lines that might easily have been shifted over to *Spectra*, published in the same year:

> I am The Man!—
> Take me, America!—the irresistible, the requisite!
> Nothing shall harm you, nothing can,
> If it results in Me.
> I am the perfect fit

For all your moods,
Shooting a slug of solid slang
Into every wall of the whole shebang . . .

It is precisely the inability to find the "perfect fit" for all his moods that tends at times to make Bynner's poems go off the rails. Yet from the beginning he possessed wit—what T. S. Eliot, in speaking of the metaphysical poets, calls "a tough reasonableness beneath the slight lyric grace." It is there, however much it owes to the Cavalier poets, in a small poem published in his first book in 1907:

Be not too frank, if you would reach
A woman's heart, be not too kind
Nor too severe, but keep your speech
And all your manners uninclined.

Assert but briefly self-control;
Then watch her come to you intent
To give direction to your soul
And make indifference different.

How much tougher this reasonableness has become in "The Edge," published in 1940:

Long, long before the eyelids harden
And an intake ends the breath,
A body's eyes and a body's burden
Feel the edge of death.

They do not move, they do not think,
They only sit and stare,
The eyes almost ceasing to blink
And the heart ceasing to care.

But it becomes a pleasant thing
To gaze upon the toes

> So peacefully dismembering
> Before the eyelids close.
>
> Thus Buddha must have sat and known,
> Midmost of earth and sea,
> The dissolution of the bone
> Into its rarity.

This poem, in its straightforward presentation in ordinary language of the universal experience of death, qualifies, to my mind, as light verse. It possesses, moreover, what T. S. Eliot terms, in speaking of Andrew Marvell's "To His Coy Mistress," that characteristic of metaphysical wit, an "alliance of levity and seriousness (by which the seriousness is intensified)." The words "pleasant" and "peacefully" in the third stanza bring the reader with totally unexpected and knife-like precision close to the edge of which the poet speaks and establish the bond of levity and seriousness that prepares him for the resolution of the final stanza.

Bynner's "Episode of Decay" presents in a similarly low-keyed and straightforward manner the picture of a woman destroying—literally devouring—her husband. The poem opens:

> Being very religious, she devoted most of her time to fear.
> Under her calm visage, terror held her,
> Terror of water, of air, of earth, of thought,
> Terror lest she be disturbed in her routine of eating her husband.

The fourth line here is one of the finest examples in modern poetry of the proper use of anticlimax. The poem continues to outline in the most matter-of-fact way, as if the poet were delivering a newscast or describing the weather, the "routine" of the woman's cannibalism. There is an elegant and unexpected choice of words: "A last valiant cell of his mind may have been insisting that the fault was not hers but his." This is black humor raised to the level of wit. On a small canvas and with the lightest touch, Bynner presents a Jamesian drama. Using words like the pale pinks and mauves in a painting by Francis Bacon, he brings his reader to contemplate with delight a scene of utter horror.

Bynner's work includes numerous examples that fit comfortably into Auden's three categories of light verse. There are epigrams and epitaphs, parodies and nonsense. In *Spectra* Emanuel Morgan's poetic forte is bathos—what D. B. Wyndham Lewis in his introduction to *The Stuffed Owl* has called the most obvious and predominant trait of good Bad Verse, "that sudden slip and swoop and slither as down a well-buttered slide, from the peaks into the abyss." (I have suggested how Witter Bynner with anticlimax, as in "Episode of Decay," learned to use this slip and swoop and slither to advantage.) Bynner's part in *Spectra* is not only a parody of the Imagists but a burlesque of the entire romantic mode. When Emanuel Morgan does not succeed, he reads like a parody of A. E. Housman or of Witter Bynner himself; when he does, he writes delightful nonsense that exists on its own merits quite apart from anything else, as in:

> If I were only dafter
>   I might be making hymns
> To the liquor of your laughter
>   And the lacquer of your limbs.
>
> But you turn across the table
>   A telescope of eyes,
> And it lights a Russian sable
>   Running circles in the skies . . .
>
> Till I go running after,
>   Obeying all your whims—
> For the liquor of your laughter
>   And the lacquer of your limbs.

1 · Introduction

Bynner found use for nonsense even in his translation of *The Way of Life According to Laotzu* (1944). "Some of the *Tao Teh Ching* sayings," he writes in his introduction to that volume, "jingle repetitively with a surface lightness like that of nursery rhymes; and I have now and then ventured such effects, besides using rhyme whenever it felt natural to the sense and stayed by the text." His social satire is amply displayed in *Cake* and *Guest Book*; and what wittier modern picture has been drawn of the politician in his public and private life than in the three lines of "A Great Man":

> Passion transforms me from my puny build . . .
> Your bosom listens to me like a crowded balcony
> To a great man speaking.

He also composed children's poems and occasional pieces. Of wit of the sort found in the *dandysme* of Laforgue there are any number of examples, such as "Fingernail":

> He had a fingernail which resembled the face of his
>   grandmother
> Who had died in her dignity before he was born
> And had bequeathed her slim grace to only one of his
>   fingers.
>
> So he chose long moments during the sunsets
> For polishing this one nail delicately and meditating
> Upon what was left him of the persistent earth.

There is also the cameo quality of Gautier, given a puritanical framework, as in "A Winter Cat-Tail":

> Cat-tail standing in the ice,
> Elderly New Englander
> Standing mirrored in the ice,
> Thin straight stalk and ruffled fur,
> Do you wonder where the wind has blown

Dandelion and golden-rod?
Or are you happier alone
With the loneliness of God?

Robert Giroux has told of T. S. Eliot in New York, when inspired by a plaque to the memory of George M. Cohan in the Oak Room of the Plaza, singing and reciting from memory the verses of any number of songs by Cohan and others, including one called "What Did Robinson Crusoe Do with Friday on Saturday Night?" Witter Bynner, who shared Eliot's love of the music hall, would have joined in. I remember listening with him in Santa Fe to an album of Anna Russell's lively and often bawdy take-offs of singers of all sorts. Bynner often improvised at the piano: inspired by the syncopated rhythms of jazz, he wrote songs for performance, as in *Cake*, or for private delectation, as in the unpublished "Arthur and Louise":

Arthur and Louise
They met one day,
Arthur and Louise
They met one day,
And she said to her man,
"You goin' away?"

And Arthur he answered
"You're nothin' but a nut,"
And Arthur he told her,
"You're nothin' but a nut,"
And Louise she answered,
"I may be—but—"

And Louise she rolled
The edge of an eye,
And Louise she rolled
The edge of an eye,
And they both got to die,
We all got to die.

Not only did Bynner compose excellent light verse throughout his career, but I would go even further and say that *all* his best work *is* light verse. His great virtue was variety; his great vice was facility. Much of what he tossed off, whether in his studio or at dinner parties, should have been tossed into the wastebasket rather than placed between covers. For me his poetry fails when it loses the internal equilibrium of wit, and veers either in one direction toward the tradition of poetry as a decorative art, or on the other toward Whitmanian magniloquence. He should have remained low-keyed and toughly reasonable, and emphasized, as Elizabeth Bishop does, his spectacular power *within* his limitations. In this way, his uniqueness would have come through more consistently. What a rich harvest he has left us all the same!

v

During my visit to Witter Bynner in November 1958, we had several long evening sessions during which I read to him and to Robert Hunt and Paul Horgan the poems that Bynner had composed as Emanuel Morgan after the disclosure of the *Spectra* hoax and which had been published in magazines or had remained over the years unpublished in his notebook. Puffing his cigar and lounging back in his chair like the contented Boston Brahmin clubman he sometimes appeared to be, Hal Bynner seemed to relish every minute of the reading. He felt, he said, that his *Doppelgänger* Morgan was again taking possession of him, and that he went to bed each night with his head filled, as it were, with the spectres of *Spectra*. He explained that while he slept complete poems came to him; on awaking he would put them down in a notebook just as he had received them. For the next months the process continued, and he soon had assembled 131 of these short pieces. They were printed just as they had come to him, without any conscious embellishment on his part.

When Bynner told me at the time what was happening, I was dubious, feeling that the enjoyment of an old joke was being carried to an absurd extreme. To inform a new generation of the hoax was one thing; to try to bring Emanuel Morgan back from the grave was another. When the volume appeared in 1960 on the eve of Bynner's eightieth birthday, I scarcely dared to read it through, fearing that it might offer little of Bynner at his best or more of Morgan at his worst. Dream creations *à la* Kubla Khan are always suspect, but in this case I need not have worried. The results that Bynner presents in this final volume, *New Poems 1960*, whatever their origin, offer the freshness and vitality found in his finest work, but with, at the same time, a new dimension.

Certainly all the events and actions in these short poems come across in the disjointed and implausible way that they would in dreams. Strange things are constantly happening: a sloth walks by an open door; a woman turns on the light and a fence disappears, leaving only the gate; doctors break a patient's jaw to try to cure his laughter, but the laugh will not be mended; a man chops up his bed for firewood and a year later it comes roaring back at him in the form of a sunset; deer speed by on their antlers; an elephant brings a third ear into the house and lays it down on the bathroom floor as a mattress.

All this reminds us of that nonsense world of Edward Lear, in which inanimate objects dart about, as indeed they do here:

> Furniture has feet too,
> > The bed the chair the sofa
> > But they walk away beyond distance
> > More kindly than people do
> > More slowly

Certain of the poems have the pure abandon and topsy-turvy nature of nonsense that any child would love:

> Two slender oysters
> > On a spring walk
> > Gossiped once
> > Out of their shells
> > And with pearls on leashes

As in the Alice books, the poems concern themselves with both sides of the mirror and with growing larger and smaller (and someone "looking at you through the wrong end of the opera-glass / And in public"). There is a fairy-tale quality to the whole with witches and palaces and a kind of subconscious Oriental ceremonial taking place:

> And then the king entered
> Followed by as many of his memories as cared
> Saluting in unison
> Like a gong

The book may be said to be a nonsense alphabet, although not consciously composed as such; the poems are arranged alphabetically according to the first word in the first line of each. They have a seemingly circular pattern to them, ending where they began, but the circle is never quite completed and we are flung back, or out, into time or endless space. The sequence—an illogical word since there is no real sequence—opens with the sea, which is itself swimming, and ends with an aged fisherman:

> You fish for people and not even their names
>   Come up for you
>
>   But the sun is still there
>   Aged fisherman
>   And you sit in it fishing for people
>   And hooking the sun

The sea is omnipresent, reminding us of the pool of tears in *Alice in Wonderland* with its evocation of the amniotic fluid. Sea creatures—otters, turtles, crocodiles—abound. There are also night creatures—moles, owls, and bats—and a mingling and reversing of day and night, just as there is a jumble of words: "Under a light he hid his bushel" and "Twice upon a time." There is throughout a preoccupation with time and timelessness, with sleep and sleepwalking. And at the heart of the book there is a terrible stillness, an inescapable loneliness:

> But all the sleep has been spoken for
> > and in the rain
>
> Months earlier
>
> And sleep was easier then
> When nobody was left alone
> When there was at least somebody
> > in the other room
> But now there is nobody anywhere
>
> He cannot find you for the life of him
> Because not even you are there
>
> That was a dream
> They come with sleep
>
> Unless you ask someone to watch

These lines read like a cry from the heart of a child or from a childlike old man, reaching out for sleep as for the comfort of death.

How much of all this is contrived? Certainly some of the images seem far too polished to have risen untouched from the depths of dream: a swallow flying backward swings "his tail forward like a cleft halberd." There is no end of deadpan humor of the sort encountered in the greenhouse explorations of the subconscious by Theodore Roethke, to which the poems appear related in subject matter, although they are wholly different in manner. The poems present a fixed form or semblance of form unlike the rhymed six-line stanzas of John Berryman's *Dream Songs*, a long poem that was begun at approximately the same time as Bynner's *New Poems*. Berryman's Dream Songs seem jagged and angular, reading at times as if played out by a semiconscious or drunken poet on a fixed piano, while Bynner's poems often give a closer sense of the free flow of dreams. What Robert Lowell said of *Dream Songs* might more aptly have been said of Witter Bynner's *New Poems 1960:* "When they don't make you cry—these poems will make you laugh. This great Pierrot's universe is more tearful and funny than we can easily bear."

Had *New Poems 1960* been published in 1961 after *The Spectra Hoax*, which brought Bynner again to attention among reviewers, it might have fared better. But coming in his eightieth year as Bynner's first volume of completely original verse in more than a decade, it went relatively unnoticed. One of the few critics to pay serious attention to it was Douglas Day in his essay "The New Old Poetry of Witter Bynner," in the Winter 1961 issue of *Shenandoah*, which is one of the few perceptive pieces of criticism of Bynner's poetry published during his lifetime.

"The only modern writer these poems call to mind is T. S. Eliot," Douglas Day writes. "When we read

> Any other time would have done
>   But not now
>   Because there is no time
>   And when there is no time
>   It only stands still on its own center
>   Waiting to be found

or (one of the best poems in the volume)

> All tempest
>   Has
>   Like a navel
>   A hole in its middle
>   Through which a gull may fly
>   in silence

we think of Eliot's still point of the turning world, timeless, quiet, and unchanging. There is in Bynner's poetry, as in *Ash Wednesday* and *Burnt Norton*, the sense that patience, humility, and introspection are the qualities that lead to the attainment of the still point. . . . The passages in Bynner's poems which evoke recollections of Eliot are, moreover, part of a theme which is seriously taken up several times in the book, and which seems indeed to be a product of the poet's subconscious: the necessary presence in life of silent recesses into which creatures can creep for quiet and solace from the confusions of the time-driven world."

In attempting to explain the formal excellence of Bynner's dream poems, Day reminds us of the years that Bynner spent on his translation of *The Jade Mountain*, the anthology of three hundred poems of the T'ang Dynasty, and of the influence they may have had. "It is possible that the strict rules of Chinese poetry have become so natural to him that his dream-visions can come neatly packaged out of his subconscious as *shih* poems of the T'ang Dynasty." Day concludes by saying that this sounds so unlikely that he half expects Bynner to announce that he has resurrected Emanuel Morgan and perpetrated a new hoax on a gullible public.

It may be, as I have suggested, that the aged Witter Bynner did indeed resurrect Emanuel Morgan, and that it was he who gave impetus to these final poems. Bynner could truthfully say in his old age, as did the young Rimbaud, *Je est Un Autre*. Yet the Other who wrote these final poems was the other self that he had spent a long time defining and tracking down, and how different that old clown was from the young perpetrator of *Spectra*.

Rereading *New Poems 1960* has given me something of a chill. The poems have about them an almost dizzying concrete, tactile quality: we seem able to reach out and touch the objects and creatures that move in and out of them. I have a sense of walking again with the old blind poet through the rooms of his house filled with their Chinese and Indian objects. I remember him one afternoon picking up the small sculpture of a bird and remarking that he liked to have things like this with him in every room so as to keep in touch with the real world.

When I finished *New Poems 1960* this last time, I afterward watched an educational television program on the subject of dinosaurs. In a matter-of-fact, deadpan manner reminiscent of Bynner's final poems, a scientist announced, "Dinosaurs did not become extinct; they simply turned into birds," and then proceeded, with the most detailed—and perhaps utterly accurate—surrealistic drawings, to illustrate his point. Hal Bynner would have erupted with laughter at that. And I thought how the old poet, in his wise way, had made us not only see and feel but also laugh until almost the end of his days.

SPECTRA

A BOOK OF POETIC

EXPERIMENTS BY

Anne Knish

AND

Emanuel Morgan

[1 9 1 6]

To Remy de Gourmont

    Poet, a wreath!—
No matter how we had combined our flowers,
You would have worn them—being ours. . . .
On you, on them, the showers—
    O roots beneath!

        Emanuel Morgan

PREFACE

This volume is the first compilation of the recent experiments in Spectra. It is the aim of the Spectric group to push the possibilities of poetic expression into a new region,—to attain a fresh brilliance of impression by a method not so wholly different from the methods of Futurist Painting.

An explanation of the term "Spectric" will indicate something of the nature of the technique which it describes. "Spectric" has, in this connection, three separate but closely related meanings. In the first place, it speaks, to the mind, of that process of diffraction by which are disarticulated the several colored and other rays of which light is composed. It indicates our feeling that the theme of a poem is to be regarded as a prism, upon which the colorless white light of infinite existence falls and is broken up into glowing, beautiful, and intelligible hues. In its second sense, the term Spectric relates to the reflex vibrations of physical sight, and suggests the luminous appearance which is seen after exposure of the eye to intense light, and, by analogy, the after-colors of the poet's initial vision. In its third sense, Spectric connotes the overtones, adumbrations, or spectres which for the poet haunt all objects both of the seen and the unseen world,—those shadowy projections, sometimes grotesque, which, hovering around the real, give to the real its full ideal significance and its poetic worth. These spectres are the manifold spell and true essence of objects,—like the magic that would inevitably encircle a mirror from the hand of Helen of Troy.

Just as the colors of the rainbow recombine into a white light,—just as the reflex of the eye's picture vividly haunts sleep,—just as the ghosts which surround reality are the vital part of that existence,—so may the Spectric vision, if successful, synthesize, prolong, and at the same time multiply the emotional images of the reader. The rays which the poet has dissociated into colorful beauty should recombine in the reader's brain into a new intensity of unified brilliance. The reflex of the poet's sight should sustain the original perception with a haunting keenness. The insubstantiality of the poet's spectres should touch with a tremulous vibrancy of ultimate fact the reader's sense of the immediate theme.

If the Spectrist wishes to describe a landscape, he will not attempt a map, but will put down those winged emotions, those fantastic analogies, which the real scene awakens in his own mind. In practice this will be found to be the vividest of all modes of communication, as the touch of hands quickens a mere exchange of names.

It may be noted that to Spectra, to these reflected experiences of life, as we perceive them, adheres often a tinge of humor. Occidental art, in contrast to art in the Orient, has until lately been afraid of the flash of humor in its serious works. But a growing acquaintance with Chinese painting is surely liberating in our poets and painters a happy sense of the disproportion of man to his assumed place in the universe, a sense of the tortuous grotesque vanity of the individual. By this weapon, man helps defend his intuition of the Absolute and of his own obscure but real relation to it.

The Spectric method is as yet in its infancy; and the poems that follow are only experimental efforts toward the desired end. Among them, the most obvious illustrations of the method are perhaps Opus 41 by Emanuel Morgan and Opus 76 by Anne Knish.

Emanuel Morgan, with whom the Spectric theory originated, has found the best expression of his genius in regular metrical forms and rhyme. Anne Knish, on the other hand, has used only free verse. We wish to make it clear that the Spectric manner does not necessitate the employment of either of these metrical systems to the exclusion of the other.

Although the members of our group would by no means attempt to establish a claim as actual inventors of the Spectric method, yet we can justifiably say that we have for the first time used the method consciously and consistently, and formulated its possibilities by means of elaborate experiment. Among recent poets in English, we have noted few who can be regarded in a sure sense as Spectrists.

Anne Knish

Anne Knish

OPUS 50

The piano lives in a dusk
Where rich amber lights
Quiver obscurely.

    It exists only at twilight;
And somewhere afar
In the depths of a tropic forest
The sun is now setting, and the phoenix looks
Mysteriously toward the gold.

    I think I must have been born in such a forest,
Or in the tangle of a Chinese screen.

    There is indigo in this music;
This dusk is filled with amber lights;
Through the tangled evening of heavy flower-scents
Come footfalls
That surely I can almost remember.

Emanuel Morgan

OPUS 41

Spectres came dancing up the wind,
    Trailing down the long grass,
Shooting high, undisciplined,
    To join the sun and see you pass . . .
    The colors of the pointed glass.

Under a willow-maze you went
    Unsaddened . . . But a violet beam
Fell on the white face, backward bent,
    Of a body in a stream.

Into the sun you came again,
    With sun-red light your feet were shod . . .
And round you stood a ring of feathered men
    With naked arms acknowledging a god.

Indigo-birds and squirrels on a tree
    And orioles flashed in and out . . .
The yellow outline of Eurydice
    Waited for Orpheus in a black redoubt.

With a beaded fern you waved away a gnat . . .
    And maidens, hung with vivid beads of green,
One of them bearing in her arms an orange cat,
    Held palms about a queen.

Then you were lost to sight
    And locking trees became the clouds of you,
Till you emerged, the moon upon your shoulder, and the night
    Bloomed blue.

Anne Knish

OPUS 76

Years are nothing;
Days alone count;
These, and the nights.
I have seen the grey stars marching,
And the green bubbles in wine,
And there are Gothic vaults of sleep.

    My cathedral
Has one great spire
Tawny in the sunlight.
Gargoyles haunt its nave;
High up amid its dark arches
Forgotten songs live shadowy.
Gold and sardonyx
Deck its altars.
Its mighty roof
Is copper rivering with the rain.

    Tomorrow lightning swords will come
And thunder of cannon.
They will unrivet this roof
Of mighty copper.
Before the eyes of my gargoyles,
In the sound of my forgotten songs,
They will take it.
And as the rain sluices down
I shall have to follow my roof into the war.

Emanuel Morgan

OPUS 15

Despair comes when all comedy
    Is tame
And there is left no tragedy
    In any name,
When the round and wounded breathing
    Of love upon the breast
Is not so glad a sheathing
    As an old brown vest.

Asparagus is feathery and tall,
And the hose lies rotting by the garden-wall.

Anne Knish

OPUS 118

If bathing were a virtue, not a lust,
I would be dirtiest.

    To some, housecleaning is a holy rite.
For myself, houses would be empty
But for the golden motes dancing in sunbeams.

    Tax-assessors frequently overlook valuables.
Today they noted my jade.
But my memory of you escaped them.

Emanuel Morgan

OPUS 7

Beyond her lips in the dark are a man's feet
    Composed and dead . . .
In the light between her lips is a moving tongue-tip sweet,
    Red.

Her arms are his white robes,
    They cover a king,
His ornaments her crescent lobes
    And two moons on a string.

Sheba, Sheba, Proserpina, Salome,
    See I am come!—king, god, saint!—
With the stone of a volcano O show that you know me,
    Pound till the true blood pricks through the paint!

Twitch of the dead man's feet if he remembers
    A bunch of grapes and a ripped-open gown.—
And the live man's eyes are night after embers,
    Two black spots on a white-faced clown . . .

And in the dawn, lava . . . rolling down . . .
Down-rolling lava on an up-pointing town.

Anne Knish

OPUS 67

I would not in the early morning
Start my mind on its inevitable journey
Toward the East.
There are white domes somewhere
Under that blue enameled sky, white domes, white
    domes;
Therefore even the cream
Is safest yellow.
Cream is better than lemon
In tea at breakfast.
I think of tigers as eating lemons.
Thank God this tea comes from the green grocer,
Not from Ceylon.

Emanuel Morgan

OPUS 13

O peacock-feather
    Drawn through a death-dim hole,
With colors blurred together,
    Persian pattern of a soul—

Is it enough to have belonged
    To the exaltation of a bird
Round whom they thronged
    Each time her high tail stirred?

. . . I loved a woman whose two eyes,
    One blue, one gray,
        Would block
Like cliffs my foothold in the skies . . .
    She is dead, they say—
        Dead as a peacock.

Anne Knish

OPUS 126

His eyes
Are the resurrection.
Once when beneath the moonrise
They looked into mine,
Grey mists held mastery between us,
And I knew that his soul
Had gone down into death.
But tonight a golden star-dust
Is pouring through space,
And the mist is burned away by it.
Tonight his soul awakens
Out of its splendid cerements,
And through his eyes the miracle
Arises to the earth.

    I have prayed long beside the tomb
And touched the grave-cloths
With living fingers.
I have lain my breasts
Against the granite
Of the sarcophagus
Where he was.
Prayers for the dead I offered up
And hecatombs.

    Today there was a wonder in the sunrise.
I knew that there were glories in the sky
And new branches of willow on the earth.
And my soul trembled with prophecy.

I prophesied
The resurrection.
Now it has come.
And I lie shaken
Before its tumult.

Emanuel Morgan

OPUS 2

Hope
Is the antelope
Over the hills;
Fear
Is the wounded deer
Bleeding in rills;
Care
Is the heavy bear
Tearing at meat;
Fun
Is the mastodon
Vanished complete . . .

And I am the stag with the golden horn
Waiting till my day is born.

Anne Knish

OPUS 151

Candle, candle,
    Flicker and flow—
I knew you once—
    But it was not long ago,
                it was

Last night.
And you spoiled my otherwise bright
                evening.

Emanuel Morgan

OPUS 62

Three little creatures gloomed across the floor
    And stood profound in front of me,
And one was Faith, and one was Hope,
    And one was Charity.

Faith looked for what it could not find,
    Hope looked for what was lost,
(Love looked and looked but Love was blind),
    Charity's eyes were crossed.

Then with a leap a single shape,
    With beauty on its chin,
Brandished a little screaming ape . . .
    And each one, like a pin,

Fell to a pattern on the rug
    As flat as they could be—
And died there comfortable and snug,
    Faith, Hope and Charity.

That shape, it was my shining soul
    Bludgeoning every sham . . .
O little ape, be glad that I
    Can be the thing I am!

Anne Knish

OPUS 131

I am weary of salmon dawns
And of cinnamon sunsets;
Silver-grey and iron-grey
Of winter dusk and morn
Torture me; and in the amethystine shadows
Of snow, and in the mauve of curving clouds
Some poison has dwelling.

    Ivory on a fan of Venice,
Black-pearl of a bowl of Japan,
Prismatic lustres of Phoenician glass,
Fawn-tinged embroideries from looms of Bagdad,
The green of ancient bronze, cinereous tinge
Of iron gods,—
These, and the saffron of old cerements,
Violet wine,
Zebra-striped onyx,
Are to me like the narrow walls of home
To the land-locked sailor.

    I must have fire-brands!
I must have leaves!
I must have sea-deeps!

Emanuel Morgan

OPUS 16

Death on a cross was not the blade
    In Mary's heart . . .
For the mother of man and the son of the maid
    Had walked one night apart,
When his beard was not yet grown—and, afraid,
    She had seen his young words dart.

Between a mother and a son,
    The guillotine . . .
It falls, it falls, and one by one,
    Unseeing and unseen,
They face the great sharp shining ton
    That time has eaten green.

Between the shoulder and the head
    The guillotine must play
And cleave with clash unmerited
    The generating clay . . .
Till the separated parts, not dead,
    Rise and walk away.

Anne Knish

OPUS 134

Listen, my friend,
That you may understand me.—

    In my earliest youth
I dreamed in hues volcanic.
I saw each day open
Like a curtain of flame.
Black slaves attended
My waking moments;
Three ebony slaves
Washed sleep from my white body.
Three ebony slaves
Around my ivory smoothness
Folded heavy robes
Of crimson and white.
And as I issued forth
Into the blue vault of the daylight
A grey ape pranced before me
And a leopard crept behind.

    This was the state
Of my young heritage.
Scarlet as the voice of trumpets
Was the pageant of my days.
Can I accept now
The twilight?
And soon the dark, where all colors
Die?

Before I die, I will hold one last revel!
I will have golden cups and poppy curtains!—
And yet—

No! . . . In a black hall
The black table shall spread far down before me
And all the feasters garbed in black.
Then, at the feast's height, I arising
Shall with a gesture like the midnight
Throw back my midnight robe and suddenly stand
Naked, the sole white flame of the world.

Emanuel Morgan

OPUS 63

The seven deathly spears of memory
Setting behind a god, a golden glorious
Halo of land and sea
Even for you and me,
    Even for us . . .

    The spear of Egypt,
Orange,
Through the sleeping lid,
With all the power of the bulk of a pyramid.

    The spear of Chile,
Yellow,
Through the thrilling cheek,
With all the push of an upturned Andean peak.

    The spear of Thibet,
Violet,
Through the eager hand,
The thrust of the iron of a silent land.

    The spear of the Ice-Poles,
Green,
Through the warm-breathing breast,
The glacial east and the glacial west.

    The spear of Norway,
Blue,
Through the curved arm-pit,
The cheerless sun majestic in a jagged slit.

    The spear of India,
Indigo,
Through the holy side,
A heaven-touching temple-roof down a mountain-slide.

    The spear of Europe,
Red,
In the mouth's breath,
The million-splintering scream of death . . .

    Even to us,
The seven-spearing sun,
The sword of separation before our love is done;
    Even for us,
A simian shape
Throwing seven souls on the sea-wet cape;
    Even for us
Who smile mouth to mouth.
The full tornado from the seven-forked south;
    Even to us
Who clasp with our knees,
The scattering upheaval of the seven cold seas!

    And this is as near as lovers ever come,
Their words are dumb;
This is as near as they have ever kissed,
Their lips are ocean-mist.

    Yet what avail the seven
Spears of memory
Against the obstinate archery
Of light, the spears of heaven?

Anne Knish

OPUS 40

I have not written, reader,
That you may read. . . .
They sit in rows in the bare school-room
Reading.
Throwing rocks at windows is better,
And oh the tortoise-shell cat with the can tied on!
I would rather be a can-tier
Than a writer for readers.

    I have written, reader,
For abstruse reasons.
Gold in the mine . . .
Black water seeping into tunnels . . .
A plank breaks, and the roof falls . . .
Three men suffocated.
The wife of one now works in a laundry;
The wife of another has married a fat man;
I forget about the third.

Emanuel Morgan

OPUS 31

The night is growing deep with snow . . .
    O put your hand in mine,
While the mirthful secrets that we know
    Bloom in the fire-shine—
Flakes falling with an undertow
    Of delicate design.

Hushed are the courts where ladies went
    Unquestioning to quaff
Goblets of liquid firmament—
    Thank God that we can laugh!

Hushed are the plains where Asia poured
    The blood of peacock kings—
But we can echo, thank the Lord,
    What the China teapot sings:

    Nothing bereaves
    The eternal tune
    Of little crisp leaves
    Green in the moon.

The night is deeper still with snow . . .
    O let us never stir
From the mirthful secrets that we know
    Of old diameter!
Eve laughed at Adam long ago,
    And Adam laughed at her.

Anne Knish

OPUS 150

Sounds, pure sounds—
Nothing—
Vibrancies of the air—
And yet—

    This summer night
There are crickets shrilling
Beyond the deep bassoon of frogs.
They cease for a moment
As the rattling clangor
Of the trolley
Bumps by.
I hear footsteps
Hollow on the pavement
Now deserted
And blank of sound.
They die.
The crickets now are sleeping;
Even the leaves
Grow still.

    And slowly
Out of the blankness, out of the silence,
Emerges on soundless wings
The long sweet-sloping
Rise and fall of far viol notes,—
The mad Nirvana,
The faint and spectral
Dream-music
Of my heart's desire.

Emanuel Morgan

OPUS 29

Knives for feet, and wheels for a chin,
And the long smooth iron bore for a neck,
And bullets for hands. . . . And the root runs in,
The root of blood no stone can check,
From the breasts of the grinding crash of sin,
From engines hugging in a wreck.

A thousand round-red mouths of pain
Blaring black,
A twisting comrade on his back
In a round-red stain,
Clotted stalks of red sumac,
Discs of the sun on a bayonet-stack . . .

Blood, flame, a cataract
Thrown upward from a desert place:
Flame and blood, the one blind fact,
Contained, or spouting from the face,
Or coiling out of bellies, packed
In a stinking spent embrace . . .
Country, a babble of black spume . . .
Faith, an eyeball in the sand . . .
Mother, a nail through a broken hand—
A kissing fume—
And out of her breast the bloody bubbling milk-red breath
Of death.

Anne Knish

OPUS 96

You are the Delphic Oracle
Of the Under-World.

    As we sit talking,
All of us together,
You flash forth sudden utterance
Of buried things
That writhe in obscure life
Within our minds' last darkness.
That which we think and say not
You say and think not.
In us these thoughts
Like worms stir vilely.
But from you they depart as sudden butterflies
Crimson and green against the pure sky.

    Many are the revelers;
Few are the thyrsus-bearers;
And sole is Dionysus.

    This I inscribe to you,
Singer,
In memory of the crags of Delphi
And the Thessalian vales beyond.

Emanuel Morgan

OPUS 40

Two cocktails round a smile,
    A grapefruit after grace,
Flowers in an aisle
    . . . Were your face.

A strap in a street-car,
    A sea-fan on the sand,
A beer on a bar
    . . . Were your hand.

The pillar of a porch,
    The tapering of an egg,
The pine of a torch
    . . . Were your leg.—

Sun on the Hellespont,
    White swimmers in the bowl
Of the baptismal font
    Are your soul.

Anne Knish

OPUS 88

So we came back again
After some years—
Just revisiting
The scenes of our sin.
Nothing is there but the garden;
And we had expected
That we would be there.

    I heard a wind blowing
Down the sky.
It came with heavy auguries
And passed.
There was a soothsayer once in Rome
Who on a white altar
Inspected the purple entrails of victims.

Emanuel Morgan

OPUS 47

Giver of bribes in the brightness of morning,
    Cities have wavered and rocked and gone down . . .
But the lamps of the altars hang round you, adorning
    The niche of your neck and the drift of your gown.

O bribe-giver, marked with purple metal—
    Cut in your naked contentment there shows
On the curve of your breast one carven petal
    From heaven's impenetrable rose!

You open the window to myriad windows,
    The high triangular door of the world . . .
Till the walls and the roofs and the curious keystone,
    The carven rose with its petals uncurled,

Are swayed in the swathe of the uppermost ether,
    Where stars are the columns upholding a dome,
And the edifice rolls on a corner of ocean,
    Lifts on a wave, poises on foam . . .

We stand on the rose, we are images golden,
    We move interchanging, attaining one crest:
One chin and one mouth and one nose and one forehead,
    One mouth and one chin and one neck and one breast . . .

I pull you apart from me, struggle to bind you,
    I free you, I rend you in seven great rays . . .
And we cling to them all . . . but we lose them, and
        slowly—
    We slip with the rainbow down the blue bays.

Anne Knish

OPUS 122

Upstairs there lies a sodden thing
Sleeping.
Soon it will come down
And drink coffee.
I shall have to smile at it across the table.
How can I?
For I know that at this moment
It sleeps without a sign of life; it is as good as dead.
I will not consort with reformed corpses,
I the life-lover, I the abundant.
I have known living only;
I will not acknowledge kinship with death.
White graves or black, linen or porphyry,
Are all one to me.
And yet, on the Lybian plains
Where dust is blown,
A king once
Built of baked clay and bulls of bronze
A tomb that makes me waver.

Emanuel Morgan

OPUS 46

I only know that you are given me
  For my delight.
No other angle finishes my soul
  But you, you white.

I know that I am given you,
  Black whirl to white,
To lift the seven colors up . . .
  Focus of light!

Anne Knish

OPUS 1

REITERATION! . . .

The seconds bob by,
So many, so many,
Each ugly in its own way
As raw meats are all ugly.
Why do we feed on the dead?
Or would at least it were with cries and lust
Of slaying our human food
Beneath a cannibal sun!
But these old corpses of alien creatures! . . .
I loathe them!
And too many heads go by the window,
All alien—
Filers of saws, doubtless,
Or lechers
Or Sabbath-keepers.
Morality comes from God.
He was busy.
He forgot to make beauty.
Why does he not call back into their hen-house
This ugly straggling flock of seconds
That trail by
With pin-feathers showing?

Emanuel Morgan

OPUS 55

Why ask it of me?—the impossible!—
    Shall I pick up the lightning in my hand?
Have I not given homages too well
    For words to understand?—

Words take you from me, bring you back again,
    Dance in our presence, cover your proud face
With the incredible counterpane,
    Break our embrace . . .

No, not to you
    Your wish,
But to some kangaroo
    Or cuttle-fish

Or octopus or eagle or tarantula
    Or elephant or dove
Or some peninsula
    Let me speak love—

Or call some battle or some temple-bell
    Or many-curving pine
Or some cool truth-containing well
    Or thin cathedral—mine!

Anne Knish

OPUS 200

If I should enter to his chamber
And suddenly touch him,
Would he fade to a thin mist,
Or glow into a fire-ball,
Or burst like a punctured light-globe?
It is impossible that he would merely yawn and rub
And say—"What is it?"

Emanuel Morgan

OPUS 17

Man-thunder, woman-lightning,
    Rumble, gleam;
Refusal,
    Scream.

Needles and pins of pain
    All pointed the same way;
Parallel lines of pain
      When the lips are gray
      And know not what they say:
Rain,
Rain.

But after the whirl of fright
    And great shouts and flashes,
    The pounding clashes
    And deep slashes,
      After the scattered ashes
Of the night,
Heaven's height
    Abashes
    With a gleam through unknown lashes
Of delicious points of light.

Anne Knish

OPUS 191

The black bark of a dog
Made patterns against the night.
And little leaves flute-noted across the moon.

    I seemed to feel your soft looks
Steal across that quiet evening room
Where once our souls spoke, long ago.

    For that was of a vastness;
And this night is of a vastness . . .

    There was a dog-bark then—
It was the sound
Of my rebellious and incredulous heart.
Its patterns twined about the stars
And drew them down
And devoured them.

Emanuel Morgan

OPUS 45

An angel, bringing incense, prays
    Forever in that tree . . .
I go blind still when the locust sways
    Those honey-domes for me.

All the fragrances of dew, O angel, are there,
The myrrhic rapture of young hair,
    The lips of lust;
    And all the stenches of dust,
Even the palm and the fingers of a hand burnt bare
    With a curling sweet-smelling crust,
And the bitter staleness of old hair,
    Powder on a withering bust . . .

The moon came through the window to our bed.
    And the shadows of the locust-tree
    On your white sweet body made of me,
    Of my lips, a drunken bee . . .
O tree-like Spring, O blossoming days,
I, who some day shall be dead,
    Shall have ever a lover to sway with me.
For when my face decays
    And the earth moulds in my nostrils, shall there not be
    The breath therein of a locust-tree,
    The seed, the shoot of a locust-tree,
    The honey-domes of a locust-tree,
    Till lovers go blind and sway with me?—

O tree-like Spring, O blossomy days,
To sway as long as the locust sways!

Emanuel Morgan

OPUS 14

Beside the brink of dream
    I had put out my willow-roots and leaves
As by a stream
    Too narrow for the invading greaves
Of Rome in her trireme . . .
Then you came—like a scream
    Of beeves.

Anne Knish

OPUS 80

Oh my little house of glass!
How carefully
I have planted shrubbery
To plume before your transparency.
Light is too amorous of you,
Transfusing through and through
Your panes with an effulgence never new.
Sometimes
I am terribly tempted
To throw the stones myself.

Emanuel Morgan

OPUS 1

They enter with long trailing of shadowy cloth,
    And each with one hand praying in the air,
And the softness of their garments is the grayness of a moth—
    The lost and broken night-moth of despair.

And they keep a wounded distance
    With following bare feet,
A distance Isadoran—
    And the dark moons beat
Their drums.

More desolate than they are Isadora stands,
    The blaze of the sun on her grief;
The stars of a willow are in both her hands,
    And her heart is the shape of a leaf.

And they come to her for comfort
    And her black-thrown hair
Is a harp of consolation
    Singing anthems in the air.

With the dark she wrestles, daring alone,
    Though their young arms would aid;
Her body wreathes and brightens, never thrown,
    Unvanquished, unafraid . . .

Till light comes leaping
    On little children's feet,
Comes leaping Isadoran—
    And the white stars beat
Their drums.

Anne Knish

OPUS 1 9 5

Her soul was freckled
Like the bald head
Of a jaundiced Jewish banker.
Her fair and featurous face
Writhed like
An albino boa-constrictor.
She thought she resembled the Mona Lisa.
This demonstrates the futility of thinking.

Emanuel Morgan

OPUS 6

If I were only dafter
    I might be making hymns
To the liquor of your laughter
    And the lacquer of your limbs.

But you turn across the table
    A telescope of eyes,
And it lights a Russian sable
    Running circles in the skies . . .

Till I go running after,
    Obeying all your whims—
For the liquor of your laughter
    And the lacquer of your limbs.

Emanuel Morgan

OPUS 9

When frogs' legs on a plate are brought to me
    As though I were divinity in France,
I feel as God would feel were He to see
    Imperial Russians dance.

These people's thoughts and gestures and concerns
    Move like a Russian ballet made of eggs;
A bright-smirched canvas heaven heaves and burns
    Above their arms and legs.

Society hops this way and that, well-taught;
    But while I watch, in cloudy state,
I feel as God would feel if He were brought
    Frogs' legs on a plate.

Anne Knish

OPUS 187

I do not know very much,
But I know this—
That the storms of contempt that sweep over us,
Ready to blast any edifice before them
Rise from the fathomless maelstrom
Of contempt for ourselves.
If there be a god,
May he preserve me
From striking with these lightnings
Those whom I love.

    Saying which,
Zarathustra strolled on
Down Fifth Avenue.

    The last three lines
Are symptomatic.

Emanuel Morgan

OPUS 104

How terrible to entertain a lunatic!
To keep his earnestness from coming close!

A Madagascar land-crab once
Lifted blue claws at me
And rattled long black eyes
That would have got me
Had I not been gay.

Anne Knish

OPUS 182

"He's the remnant of a suit that has been drowned;
That's what decided me," said Clarice.
"And so I married him.
I really wanted a merman;
And this slimy quality in him
Won me.
No one forbade the banns.
Ergo—will you love me?"

Emanuel Morgan

OPUS 101

He not only plays
One note
But holds another note
Away from it—
As a lover
Lifts
A waft of hair
From loved eyes.

The piano shivers,
When he touches it,
And the leg shines.

Anne Knish

OPUS 181

Skeptical cat,
Calm your eyes, and come to me.
For long ago, in some palmed forest,
I too felt claws curling
Within my fingers . . .
Moons wax and wane;
My eyes, too, once narrowed and widened . . .
Why do you shrink back?
Come to me: let me pat you—
Come, vast-eyed one . . .
Or I will spring upon you
And with steel-hook fingers
Tear you limb from limb. . . .

There were twins in my cradle. . . .

Emanuel Morgan

OPUS 78

I am beset by liking so many people.
What can I do but hide my face away?—
Lest, looking up in love, I see no eyes or lids
In the gleaming whirl of clay,
Lest, reaching for the fingers of love,
I know not which are they,
Lest the dear-lipped multitude,
Kissing me, choke me dead!—

O green eyes in the breakers,
White heave unquieted,
What can I do but dive again, again—again—
To hide my head!

Anne Knish

OPUS 135

In a tomb of Argolis,
Under an arch of great stones,
Where my eyes were sightless, groping,
I touched this figment of clay.

    Forgotten vase of immemorial Greece,
Colorless form!
I have entered to the blind dark
Of the tomb where you have slept forever
And with the dreams of my importunate hands
I touch you in the profound darkness.

    You are cold and estranged;
Yet the ends of my fingers cling to your porous surface.
You are thin and very tall;
My palm can cover your mouth.
Your lip curves but a little;
Around your throat
My two hands meet,
And then part as I follow the swelling
Rhythm that downward widens,
And I pass around and under,
And the returning line
Ebbs home.

Beneath your feet I touch cold marble;
My hand returns
To sleep upon your breast
Dreaming it warm.

Emanuel Morgan

OPUS 79

Only the wise can see me in the mist,
    For only lovers know that I am here . . .
After his piping, shall the organist
    Be portly and appear?

Pew after pew,
    Wave after wave . . .
Shall the digger dig and then undo
    His own dear grave?

Hear me in the playing
    Of a big brass band . . .
See me, straying
    With children hand in hand . . .

Smell me, a dead fish . . .
    Taste me, a rotten tree. . . .
Someday touch me, all you wish,
    In the wide sea.

LATER SPECTRIC POEMS

A SELECTION

[1 9 1 7 – 1 9 2 7]

Anne Knish

OPUS 371

The tawny plexus, the animate focus, of infinite luminous rays,
Moving across the street
In the golden nimbus of light—
Reflecting, refracting, identifying
The flooding waves of ether:
It is an irony of the curled smiling Gods
That light, leaving the sun,
Should travel a hundred million miles
In adventure of desolate space, lonely and perilous,
To splinter and disintegrate at last
Against a street-cur.

Anne Knish

OPUS 344

    My lust of roundness will betray me
Into the arms of God, some day.

    And I shall feel that I have cheated the Devil
If at the end of life
I have concealed from him how well I could be tempted
By triangles.

    As for the rest, my whole life seems a long
Effort to circumvent and overleap
And crawl beneath all manner of polygons,
Squares, rhomboids, parallelograms.
At night I dream that cubes are crushing me;
And a free octagon, if I should meet it,
Would strike me dead.

Elijah Hay

NIGHT

    I opened the door
And night stared at me like a fool,
Heavy dull night, clouded and safe—
I turned again toward the uncertainties
Of life within doors.

    Once night was a lion,
No, years ago night was a python
Weaving designs against space
With undulations of his being—
Night was a siren once.

    Oh sodden middle-aged night,
I hate you!

Emanuel Morgan

OPUS 88

The drunken heart finds epics on the breast-bone
    of a chicken
And lyrics under the lettuce.

The drunken heart
Sings a song of sixpence.
You are the emptying bottle of rye, beloved,
You are also the next bottle.

The drunken heart
Is as full of hops as a green grasshopper . . .
The heart is as full of hops
As a red squirrel . . .
There is a stone-wall, leading to a motherly tree
Which clicks with the flickering caress
And parts for the leap.
And you, beloved,
Are a nut.

Morgan and Knish

PRISM ON THE PRESENT
STATE OF POETRY

Knish:—
   Out of a cradling has there come a sunset?
Oh for the fellowship when once in Alexandria
The world of learning burned!

Morgan:—
   Laughter, dear friends, will do for kindling;
And we shall wear ridiculous beads of flame
To tinkle toward the corners of the world,
Slapping with light the faces of old fools.

Elijah Hay

ELIJAH CELEBRATES FOR EMANUEL

If only my thoughts were dolphins, fat and free,
Untaught by morals and uncurbed by speech,
Fresh as the waves that tumble on the beach,
I could be gay, inconsequentially.
My thoughts are more like anchovies, I see
How rigid, tail in mouth, linked each to each
Immutably and logically they reach,
The present, past and future thoughts of me!

Anne Knish

I

    I once knew a man
Who had on his parlor table
An eighteen-inch plaster statuette called
"Leaving home."

    And in the window-niche in the hall
Was another figure
Called "Baby's First Flower."

    When he died
We buried these two with him;
For they had all three been dead
A long time.

11

TO EMANUEL

    O poet, O vile one!
Crawling through key-holes
And slithering up lightning rods
To evoke the fly-swatter
And the thunder-stroke—
You exist in an ever fresh confusion
Of punched papers and rusting steel girders
And your own effluvia.
I would I were a little bird
That I might fly away.

Emanuel Morgan

THESE GULLS

These gulls look more to me like lima-beans.
What difference anyway
Whether a beak and wings add to the contour
Or a pod and vine?
A round belly can lie
Quietly parallel
To the round edge of the earth.
And yet after all
You whom I love
Look to me like me.
And this becomes you.

Emanuel Morgan

THE LITTLE REVIEW

(In the editorial office of The Little Review
*were Margaret Anderson, Harriet Dean and
Caesar Swaska, the two editors and the office boy.)*

    Three in a dark room,
    A tulip,
    A chocolate,
    A candle with no holder, lighting
    A Victory with no head.

Emanuel Morgan

WORDS

You have words
But nothing hangs on them.
On the moulding of your mouth they gleam
Like empty picture-hooks.

Emanuel Morgan

SPANISH GOLD

The manifold
Red lustre of your hair, ringing like a bell,
Made, when you moved, a most delicious din—
As of Spanish gold
Brought red and shining with a deep-sea spell
Up from the depths of sin.

Emanuel Morgan

TO A HARASSED YOUNG MAN

Rinse out that woman's eyes!
They hang on you
Like a washcloth
On a hook.

Emanuel Morgan

DETROIT

Centipede city,
Each little foot is a motor car
Speeding in many directions,
And the whole body
Slips forward
To the heaven of centipedes,
To the enormous feedings,
Under a sun
Obscured by the smoky breath
Of too much.

But if a pyramid
Large enough
Were built of the legs of centipedes,
It would as nearly reach the moon,
Where there is nothing,
As would a heap
Of blonde combings
Of butterfly wings.

Therefore, revolve,
Little legs,
Therefore, great city,
Move on!

Emanuel Morgan

THE BLIND PIG

Now comes a cocktail
And rests in a cranny—
Apple-pie order, a fig for your granny!

People go round us
In slices of eight—
Why haven't we eaten?—why do we wait?

What if he bring us
Another one? Can he?
Apple-pie order, a prune for your granny!

There once was a star
On the top of a tree,
Pointed with features of you and of me.

Your words are Choctaw,
Mine Hindoostanee—
Apple-pie order, a fig for your granny!

Emanuel Morgan

JACKSTRAWS

Picking up jackstraws,
They called themselves athletes.

Emanuel Morgan

MONSTER

The monster,
Ringletted with perfumes,
Utters, above clouds,
A growling chirp,
While all the birds of heaven scatter
In close pairs.

Emanuel Morgan

PEANUTS

If you must do it,
Make it cocoanuts.
Let there be milk in your madness,
Choose a big one—
Like Hamlet's father.

Emanuel Morgan

EASE

I have escaped into the hump of a dromedary,
There to be flopped along
With no responsibility.

POSTHUMOUS POEMS OF EMANUEL MORGAN

*(On hearing from Budapest of
the death of Anne Knish from an obscure
disease, Emanuel Morgan committed suicide
at a sanitarium in Pittsburgh.)*

[1 9 2 7]

Emanuel Morgan

OPUS 111

I laid the griffin's egg
And you are hatching it—
And this is your spectrum,
Anne Knish.

The staircase, the landing, the upper-hall carpet,
Are calling you mother.
You are weary of the desert-sanded rung,
The grown and withered words—
But the upper-hall carpet
Is calling you mother.

After the end
Comes always the beginning . . .
And when you begin to understand this,
I shall have done with meaning it.

Emanuel Morgan

OPUS 113

Enormous and terrible surf,
For all the years of your charging,
I lie on the sand
More troubled by a fly.

Enormous and terrible surf,
There are life-guards
But not for me.

For if you came near me with your shout,
I should but rise and walk away—
And the fly would follow.

Emanuel Morgan

OPUS 107

She clung to me close as water in a pool
And sharp as thunder of the night—
And every pulse of me, rushing out of school,
Shouted delight.

She clung to me close as a river-soaked shirt
And sharp as a sliver under a nail
Till every nerve in me slunk away hurt
And hung its tail.

Emanuel Morgan

FRAGMENT

Whether I be a mountain to climb
Or a puddle to look into—
Look,
Take your time.

PINS FOR WINGS

BY

Emanuel Morgan

[1920]

To William Marion Reedy

1 8 6 2 – 1 9 2 0

A mirror breathed upon by Death
but undimmed

Æ

liquid air
somewhere

Conrad Aiken

phosphorescent
plumbing

Richard Aldington

an Attic vase
full of tea

Katherine Lee Bates

four-and-twenty blackbirds
half-baked in a pie

Stella Benson

Cinderella's
riding-breeches

Maxwell Bodenheim

a tooth
toe-dancing

William Aspenwall Bradley

a bearded wheel-
barrow

Gelett Burgess

sculptured chewing-gum
on a trolley

Witter Bynner

God
in the sugar-bowl

Bliss Carman

little hills
tipping their hats

Gilbert K. Chesterton

a Cardinal
on a merry-go-round

Sarah N. Cleghorn

the rosy half
of an old apple

Padraic Colum

the whistle of a kettle
to the petal of a thistle

Alice Corbin

a quiver
full of rulers

E. E. Cummings

much ado
about the alphabet

Gabriele D'Annunzio

a passion-flower
dipped in ammonia

Walter de la Mare

a door-knob
in the mist

Babette Deutsch

the phoenix
lays a purple bomb

Max Eastman

Aphrodite
tattooed on a muscle

T. S. Eliot

the wedding cake
of two tired cultures

John Erskine

marbles
in a muff

Donald Evans

the necktie
of Lucifer

Arthur Davison Ficke

St. Sebastian
in gloves
trimming his arrow-tips

John Gould Fletcher

two halves of a typewriter
still moving

Robert Frost

paintings by the family
in birch-bark frames

Robert Graves

a khaki bib

Edgar Guest

communion-bread
with slices of bologna

Hermann Hagedorn

the silver lining
of the Y. M. C. A.

Elijah Hay

lather
but no beard

Oliver Herford

bottled kittens

Ford Madox Hueffer

a grey-hound
loping with pugs

H.D.

the Winged Victory
hopping

Robinson Jeffers

Aimee Semple McPherson
in a thunderstorm

Orrick Johns

the Rubaiyat
carved on a carrot

Rudyard Kipling

Pan
stoking an empire

Anne Knish

a gargoyle
remembering

Alfred Kreymborg

Pierrot
with the hiccoughs

D. H. Lawrence

lovers
eating thistle-pie

Richard Le Gallienne

talcum-powder on the
tail of a wayward
nightingale

Amy Lowell

a rhinestone chip
on a blood-red shoulder

Maurice Maeterlinck

a dreamy fat man
dancing
in blue gauze

Edwin Markham

he has learned the art
of leaning on a hoe
without soiling his beard

Don Marquis

a walnut bureau
with crickets for handles

Edna St. Vincent Millay

a hamadryad
in the tree of knowledge

Harriet Monroe

the Mother Superior
considers lingerie

Angela Morgan

Jeanne d'Arc
seizes a trombone

Emanuel Morgan

a bat
and a butterfly
mating

Gilbert Murray

a discus-thrower
perfumed

Yone Noguchi

incense
for breakfast

Ezra Pound

a book-worm
in tights

Edwin Ford Piper

a heart-beat
in a hen-house

Robert Alden Sanborn

back-scratchers
in bloom

Carl Sandburg

a snow-pudding
of fists

George Santayana

a withered
rose-window

Odell Shepard

spring-wind
up the trouser-leg

J. C. Squire

a ballet
of marshmallows

Gertrude Stein

wings rotting
under water

Wallace Stevens

the shine of a match
in an empty pipe

Charles Wharton Stork

stilts
clasping

Arthur Symons

enchanted
Roquefort

Charles Hanson Towne

church-bells
on a bicycle

Louis Untermeyer

Paris
awarding the apple
to Vulcan

Henry Van Dyke

a pulpit
slowly waltzing

George Sylvester Viereck

a palanquin
on a dachshund

Arthur Waley

woollen gloves
assorting feathers

John Hall Wheelock

a floral display
in an ice-cream parlor

William Carlos Williams

carbolic acid
in love

George Edward Woodberry

grape-juice
in the Holy Grail

Edith Wyatt

a cornstalk
held up with a hairpin

William Butler Yeats

a pot of mould
at the foot of the rainbow

CAKE

AN INDULGENCE

[1 9 2 6]

CHARACTERS

[In the Order of Their Appearance]

PROLOGUE
The Unicorn

ACT I
The Lady
The Cake-Servant
Eight Other Servants
A Psychoanalyst
Mary Magdalen
A Messenger-Boy
Judas
Adam
Eve
Nine Angels
An Artist

ACT II
A Mandarin
Two Coolies

ACT III
A Negro
A Camera-Man

ACT IV
A Swami
A Disciple
Passers-by

The music should be trumpet, trombone, oboe, clarinet, tympani and piano.

PROLOGUE

THE UNICORN

(A suave and portly Chamberlain, appearing before the curtain and carrying his horn as a staff of office)

Ladies and gentlemen, it will save us trouble,
Because a number of us have to double
And none of you like to come at eight-fifteen,
If you will let us cut the opening scene.
The scene was not so good, as a matter of fact,
And only complicated the first act.
It was added by the author to allow
People to come in late, as they're doing now;
But the management prefers this simpler way
Of trying to connect you with the play.
And between ourselves, the company, being nervous,
Believed this opportunity might serve us
To let you know that we have never quite
Approved of what we offer you tonight.
It hasn't any plot in the usual sense,
There's nothing pivotal, there's nothing tense.
I hope I haven't given the thing away.
This isn't at all what I was asked to say,
And I must do my best to make amends.
I therefore beg you to imagine, friends,
A sort of drawing-room, with coal-black drapes
And drooping lights covered with purple grapes.
The Lady the play's about is giving a tea,

Assisted by her Chamberlain, that's me.
The Lady herself is sitting in the middle,
And they're listening to a fellow with a fiddle.
Then everybody talks and no one hears,
And the Lady sits in the middle, bored to tears.
That was the scene. It wasn't very much,
Except that it was done with a modern touch,
You know the sort of thing, nobody there,
Each of the guests was just an empty chair,
And we had the members of the orchestra play
Things that the empty chairs were supposed to say.
Some people thought it was funny, but it wasn't.
It's a play that either gets you, or it doesn't,
As you may judge for yourselves in just a minute.
I'm hoping that it does—because I'm in it.

ACT I

(On a Height of Gold at the back of the stage sits a LADY. *Her throne is a gilded eagle with wings spread forward; her background a tapestry of heaven against which hangs, like a nimbus, a great gong of brass. She is resting her elbow on an eagle-wing, her chin wearily on her thumb and fingers. She wears an exaggerated coronet of golden eagles. In fact everything about the* LADY *and her court is overdone, except the two chairs, one on each side of her throne, which are low and supported by dollar-signs couchants. In one of them sits the* UNICORN, *her Chamberlain, reading a newspaper. To the left stands a handsome and very young* SERVANT *with a tray of exaggerated buns and pastries. Three other* SERVANTS *are in attendance.)*

THE LADY

The trouble with me is I'm bored with being bored.
How long this living takes! How long, O Lord!
I have had seven husbands—and that's enough, I think.
I have come through mysticism, free love, and drink.
I am offered everything money can buy,
And yet there's nothing I want—not even to die.

THE UNICORN

(With a blow on the gong)
The smelling salts!

THE LADY

(Restraining one of the SERVANTS, *with an indifferently raised hand)*

Am I Victorian,
To be given a sniff of tears by any man?
The world has moved, since women kept their hearts
As sticky as a dish of apple tarts.
It's different now: I know what I'm about;
I am a modernist. I am tired out.
I must find me a chamberlain who understands!

THE UNICORN

(Hastily)
Shall it be psycho-analysis?—or glands?

THE LADY

Order me everything that you can think of.
There isn't a liquor left I want a drink of.
Order me anything. I'm desperate!

THE UNICORN

There's a famous doctor below. I had him wait.
What ho! Bring on the Psychoanalyst!
    (He strikes the gong. Four additional SERVANTS *bring into the Presence the* PSYCHOANALYST, *a tiny man with not enough beard to conceal his thin neck.)*

THE PSYCHOANALYST

(Going straight to the LADY*)*
Yes, I can see at once that you resist.

THE LADY

I don't.

THE PSYCHOANALYST

You've proved it. Let me feel your dream!
    (Feeling her pulse)
Your need of psychospection is extreme.
Turn over on the other dream a minute.

(She turns over, he puts his ear on her heart and then beckons the UNICORN.*)*
Just listen to the indican that's in it!
And the subconscious, bearing all the brunt!
(To the LADY*)*
Do you dream better on your back or front?

THE LADY

The latter.

THE PSYCHOANALYST

Then your case is very clear.
You need to live a while on the frontier.

THE LADY

And dine on pork and beans? I won't go there.

THE PSYCHOANALYST

You'll have a nervous breakdown.

THE LADY

I don't care.

THE PSYCHOANALYST

O Lady, you are doing very wrong!
Do you want to know what made me big and strong?

THE LADY

(Amazed)
Were you ever any smaller?

THE PSYCHOANALYST

Well, I'm lean;
But I've changed a twelve-size collar for fourteen,
All in a month, since I have learned to go
Two or three times a day to a picture-show.

I hated the movies once, I used to cry
When I had to visit them. The reason why?
In love with Mary Pickford, that was all,
And used to try to cure it with baseball.
I even told myself she wasn't pretty.
But now I travel, city after city,
To see a Pickford picture and I write
A love-letter to Mary every night.
Today my heart makes only happy sounds,
And Lady, I have gained eleven pounds.

    THE LADY

What has all this to do with me?

    THE PSYCHOANALYST

Your case is different. Let me see.

    THE LADY

I'm bored with him. Pay him his fee.

    THE PSYCHOANALYST

  (Thoughtful)
To loosen up your frontier libido,
I recommend for you—

    THE LADY

  (Peremptory)
Please go.

    THE PSYCHOANALYST

  (Resentful)
You're frivolous. I might have known—

    THE LADY

You leave my libido alone!
  (Four SERVANTS *abruptly remove the aggrieved Specialist.)*

THE LADY

I want some cake, give me some cake,
No, not cake, bread with raisins.
No, not bread with raisins,
I want some cake. Give me some cake.
> (*The* CAKE-SERVANT *advances with his tray; she selects a large piece of cake.*)

THE UNICORN

Why did you take it?

THE LADY

Because it was there.

THE UNICORN

I ask, merely to be asking.

THE LADY

I eat, merely to be eating—
Not that I care.

THE UNICORN

> (*Crossing to the other chair*)

I spoke that you might hear the sound of my voice,
To prove that you are not alone in the world,
That you have me beside you.

THE LADY

If you were not beside me,
I should be beside myself.

THE UNICORN

You show a gift for words, my Lady.
You should write.

THE LADY

Yes, that might help me.
What shall I write?

THE UNICORN

You must have experience
To be able to write.

THE LADY

I have had seven husbands!

THE UNICORN

You have had the ordinary life of the modern woman,
But that's not experience.
You must have experience.

THE LADY

(Eagerly)
Bring me some experience.

THE UNICORN

What ho, experience!
> *(He strikes the gong. Eight* SERVANTS *enter, four from each side, and bow to her in a semi-circle.)*

THE LADY

(Annoyed)
But this is not experience,
This is what I have every day.
I want something strange, something different.

THE UNICORN

(To the SERVANTS*)*
Reverse!
> *(Instantly the* SERVANTS *turn about, facing away from her, and bow, encircling her with their rears.)*

THE UNICORN

You may now see things from a different point of view.

THE LADY

But this is only a symbol of experience.
These are my servants, they are bought and paid for,
And I have heard that experience may not be bought and paid for.

THE UNICORN

Paid for, Lady, but not bought.
  (*To the* SERVANTS)
Reverse!
  (*They turn about, facing her, and bowing again.*)

THE LADY

  (*To the* SERVANTS)
You may go now, no, I want something,
I want some cake, no, not cake, bread with raisins,
No, not bread with raisins,—
  (*Helplessly*)
What is it I want?

THE UNICORN

You were about to invite experience.

THE LADY

Ah, that was it! I want two writing-desks.
  (*To the* SERVANTS)
Bring pens and ink, blotters and envelopes,
Parchment and sealing-wax and my signatures.
We shall invite experience.
What shall I do with this cake?
I knew that I shouldn't have taken it.
If it had been raisin-bread—
I shouldn't have known either.

THE UNICORN

(To the SERVANTS*)*
Cut it into eight pieces,
And divide it among the eight bird-cages.
This is what is known as charity.
> *(A* SERVANT *removes from the scene the piece of cake. The other* SERVANTS *leave on their errands. The* UNICORN *looks at his newspaper.)*

THE LADY

(Aside)
Though he'd like to be fonder
Of an amorous caper,
His attentions wander
To the morning paper.
He has tripped with no trollops,
Practised no sin—
And yet there are collops
Under his chin.

THE UNICORN

(Aside)
She has had her Peking puppies, ponies and marmosets,
Now she is out for larger game, for more important pets.
But, after all, she pays for what she gets.

THE LADY

If you would turn your head this way, I could hear you.

THE UNICORN

(With self-discipline)
Reverse!
> *(He reverses and faces her. The* SERVANTS *return, bearing the objects commanded, objects larger and stranger than usual.)*

THE LADY

One desk for him, and one for me.
We shall compose. What shall we compose?

THE UNICORN

We shall compose, first of all, ourselves.

THE LADY

(After rising, smoothing the velvet cushion of her throne and sitting again)
I am composed.
Now write something
For me to make important with my signature.

THE UNICORN

Why not the signature and nothing else?
It would be most impressive.

THE LADY

Because, unless I keep you occupied,
You read the newspaper, you rattle it,
You wrap your brain in newspaper.

THE UNICORN

I wrap my brain in newspaper, Lady,
In order to keep out moths.
How could I approach your signature
With a head full of holes?

THE LADY

Let us do what we were doing.
What were we doing?

THE UNICORN

(Arranging sheets of paper and three carbons)
We were sending out an announcement.

THE LADY
Of what?

THE UNICORN

Of you—to whom it may concern
Or not, as the case may be.
I will repeat as you dictate.
(Reading, as he composes with a long vermilion pen)
I am a Lady who has never cared,
I have had everything,
I was born in a rich man's pocket
Of his wedding-ring,
I am not a lady of autumn,
But a lady of spring
Who has never really experienced
Anything.
I desire to know what life is like,
What the days and nights may bring,
So please do all that you can for one
Who has met the British King.
My Chamberlain has taken down
Exactly what I have said.
I want to buy experience.
Dictated, but not read.

THE LADY

(Lifting the objects as she names them)
Pen, bring me something different.
Ink, bring me something strange.
Paper, bring me something mysterious.
Blotter, bring me something that no one else has experienced.
Servant, bring me my signature to copy.
(A SERVANT brings her a large flourishing signature)

THE UNICORN

(Laying the letters on the desk before her)
If you intend to write, my Lady,
It might be well, first of all, to learn your own signature.

THE LADY

(Signing the first)
I know my own signature,
But in so many different styles
That I never know which to prefer.

THE UNICORN

Will you know, then, which experience to prefer?
You cannot have experience brought back to you to copy.

THE LADY

(Signing the second)
Oh yes, I can. When I lie in bed in the morning,
It will all come back to me and I shall write it down.
   (Signing the third)
Or perhaps I shall not write it down,
Perhaps I shall just dream about it.
After all, why write?

THE UNICORN

After all, why dream?

THE LADY

(Signing the fourth)
Perhaps I shall not dream at all
But just go on experiencing
What nobody else has experienced.
They're signed. Please have them sent.

THE UNICORN

*(Taking the scripts and handing each of the four
to a* SERVANT)
To the four corners of the earth, four couriers!
This one to France, this one to China,
This one to Africa and this to India.
And ask each corner kindly to supply—

THE LADY

The very best experience money can buy.
    (As the four SERVANTS *bow)*
Reverse!
    (They bow backwards and go their four ways.)

THE UNICORN

    (Sagely)
To see life steadily and see it whole—

THE LADY

    (To the CAKE-SERVANT*)*
Bring me, please, a jelly-roll.
    (The handsome young CAKE-SERVANT *serves her, but she notices none of her servants.)*
    (Darkness.)
    (An interlude of Parisian music.)
    (The risen Curtain reveals the UNICORN *looking down from the edge of the Height and the* LADY, *astride a cardboard steamer, descending an unfolded ladder into a Parisian Boulevard.)*

THE UNICORN

    (Gesticulating with a newspaper)
Paris! Paris! No wonder you were named for the youth
Who satisfied even Helen with her sweet tooth!
    (Taking the steamer back from the LADY*)*
The sophisticated smell of the air,
Beguiling a lady to be debonair!
The lights of the boulevard, the en passant Maupassant dash!
You will meet a young man with a small moustache,
Corruptly pale, romantically thin,
Who will narrow his eyes to a demi-tasse of after-dinner sin!
You will meet artists who have come here to learn the art of
    paint

From harlots. You are meeting now the only saint
Worth mention among men.
> (*A young woman enters the Boulevard, in Parisian dress but with a halo on her coil of red hair. The* UNICORN *retires to a comfortable position on the* LADY's *throne, where he relaxes with a cigarette and his newspaper.*)

THE LADY

Lend me your halo, Mary Magdalen?

MARY

> (*Sadly*)

I am always lending everything I own.
It's a marvel that I have been able to keep my flesh and bone
From the collectors for their museums. But I have heard that my
    poet will come back again,
Back to his beloved, back to his Magdalen.
And so I go on these nineteen hundred years,
Wondering if I shall know him when he appears,
And so I go on, looking among all these thousands of faces and
    eyes—
And they are all lies.

THE LADY

You know that you are enjoying yourself.

MARY

I am not.

THE LADY

If you're not, you ought to be.

MARY

Well, perhaps in a way I am.
> (*Curtains of Stars are drawn across the Height and the* UNICORN *is forgotten.*)

THE LADY

Do you leave heaven often?

MARY

Take a thousand wrong turns on the earth and one right one,
That interns you in heaven.
Take in heaven eternal right turns and one wrong one,
That returns you to earth.

THE LADY

May a wrong turn be taken in heaven?

MARY

With the flip of a wing.

THE LADY

How comforting!
I had always thought of heaven as a single long street
With the angels going all one way and nobody to meet.

MARY

Oh, no, there are many turnings,
And each of them is supposed to be more beautiful than any
    of them.
In early days when the immigration laws were lax,
The order of the turnings was carefully numbered;
And, by counting the numbers and watching your step,
You could go on and never come to an end of ever more
    beautiful turnings.
But now that the bar of heaven has been put up,
And there are quotas from the various countries,
And a consequent lack of new angels to take care of the numbers
Which the old angels are too proud of to take care of,
The numbers have been wearing off and falling down—
So that everybody in heaven is going a little bit wrong
And being suspended back to earth like me.

THE LADY

(Hopefully)
Exactly what had you done?

MARY

I had gone a little bit wrong with St. Peter.

THE LADY

Only a little bit?

MARY

I had chucked him under the chin,
And he had turned the other chin,
And St. Bridget had to see me chuck him under the other chin.
But he let me bring my halo.

THE LADY

Were there no younger angels, with fewer chins?

MARY

I chucked him under the chin because it itches there
From leaning so long on the gate.

THE LADY

And he didn't like it?

MARY

Yes, but I had no business to be tender-hearted.
Itches are forbidden in heaven.

THE LADY

Can you ever go back?

MARY

My time is up now—but not if I know it.
I'll stay here and show them, I'll stay here and wait for my poet.

THE LADY

That suits me exactly. I'll go in your place.

MARY

Mistake you for me?

THE LADY

If I cover my face?

MARY

How could you cover it?

THE LADY

Boy!
   (*As a* MESSENGER *enters*)
A dozen scarlet switches!
   (*As the* BOY *goes out*)
Taking your tip for my heavenly trip, I shall pay no attention to itches.

MARY

(*Handing the* LADY *her halo*)
Very well. My halo. My name.
The same old game,
Though they told me when they gave me this, that I never must consign it.

THE LADY

(*Examining it*)
I shall have a servant shine it.

MARY

I knew I ought not to be lending it!
What if your servant, in shining it, should be bending it?

THE LADY

(*Putting it on and bending it, with the aid of a vanity-case mirror*)
Just a little bit here
By the ear.
A prettier line.
Why don't you bob your hair like mine?

MARY

Give me my halo.

THE LADY

(*Disregarding*)
You attach too much importance, my dear, to things.

MARY

When I left heaven, I left my wings—

THE LADY

Behind you for Paris, everyone does.

MARY

And when he comes back, he will find me as I was.

THE LADY

Faith is an excellent drug for those who choose it.
He will never come back. Give me that tear,
I can use it.
(*She applies the tear-drop to her hair with her finger-tip, not noticing the entrance of a walking-stick and a dapper young Parisian with a small moustache.*)

THE LADY

I seem to feel a shadow. What can have subdued us?

MARY

(*Seeing him*)

It's Judas.

THE LADY

That beautiful person, Judas? Oh, my dear!

JUDAS

(Approaching her)
Do you hold it against me?

THE LADY

(Cordially)
The halo?

JUDAS

No, the sin.

THE LADY

Lift up your chin.
Let me look at your throat. Not a sign of a scar!
You can't be, you're not! Are you sure that you are?

JUDAS

I'd rather have been Judas than any of the others.
Who wishes to think of all men as his brothers?

THE LADY

Not I. God forbid.

JUDAS

Then you think as I did.
And notice, my dear, we're in Paris, not Hades.
   (As MARY begins to weep)
Thank God you're not one of these lachrymose ladies
Crying, like Mary, for thousands of years,
And living, like camels, on their own tears.
   (The MESSENGER-BOY returns with red switches. THE LADY fastens them into her bobbed hair.)

JUDAS

Bobbed hair going out?

THE LADY

Long hair coming in.
Lend me some, Mary. I haven't a pin.
(She borrows hair-pins from MARY, *whose red hair is thus loosened and falls long.)*

JUDAS

(Loudly)
Let's go and dine. It's long after seven.

THE LADY

I can't go to dinner. I'm going to heaven.
(A great hook comes out and drags the LADY *off the Boulevard.)*

JUDAS

"Let's go and dine" was a cue for the students.
I've told 'em to act with decorum and prudence.

MARY

The halo worked.

JUDAS

It always works—
The sanctification of feminine quirks.

MARY

Here comes the model, dressed as Eve.

JUDAS

(Looking off)
A Creation, I call it. And yet, I believe,
She's made a mistake in her costume for heaven.

(Calling to her)
Cover your navel, Eve oughtn't to have one.

EVE

(Entering, rearranging her leaves)
Now how do I look?

JUDAS

You look like sin.

EVE

Good. It's the business I'm supposed to be in.

MARY

Where's Adam?

EVE

Undressing.

JUDAS

The angels?

EVE

They're ready.
But only four white ones, the fifth was unsteady.
Has the victim come through?

JUDAS

We'll collect by-and-by.
Enough for us all. Go on back to the sky.
   (As EVE *obeys)*
What fools American women be!
We'll give her a taste of gay Paree!
   (A tinkle of harps is heard.)

MARY

O Matthew, Mark, O Luke and John,
I hear a harp! The show is on.
> *(Darkness)*
> *(After music, fanfaring with trumpets and pealing with thunder, light reveals on the Height a starry space and a row of* FOUR WHITE ANGELS, *two of them on each side of a great angel-cake. They are playing softly when the* LADY *enters heaven from behind the Choir, her red switches across her face.)*

THE LADY

I have returned.
> *(Indignant because no attention is paid to her)*

Oughtn't there to be more joy in heaven over the one sinner
Than over—especially when I gave up a most attractive
    invitation to dinner?
> *(Insistent, as they continue to play)*

I have come back again.
I am Mary Magdalen.
> *(And still they play, while Adam and Eve enter, dressed in leaves, he carrying a drum, she a tambourine.)*

THE LADY

(Briskly)
How different! Why don't you dress in robes like the others?

ADAM

(With a drum-beat)
We wouldn't if we had 'em.
Eve is original.

EVE

(With a tambourine-shake)
So is Adam.

ADAM

Of course in being original our specialty was sin.

EVE

But that was the most original that we have ever been.

THE LADY

It seems to be original here, merely to speak.

ADAM

You mustn't blame the young ones. They've been singing till they're weak.

EVE

Adam and I are fortunate. Having lived here longer than they
And knowing every inch of heaven, we never lose our way;
But these poor dears are terrified of everything but song.

THE LADY

What can they be afraid of here?

ADAM

Afraid of going wrong.

EVE

Some of the angels are mutinous, they have meetings every night.

ADAM

They demand permission to turn to the left, when they ought to turn to the right.

THE FOUR WHITE ANGELS

(Stroking their harps)
Sing, sing, what shall we sing?
A Red ran away with a harpsichord string!

They break up our practice and try, every night,
To make us go wrong when we want to go right.
>   (EVE *peers closely at the* LADY, *then whispers to* ADAM.)

ADAM

>   *(Repulsing her)*

No need of whispering anything here.
I don't get a word and you tickle my ear.
>   *(A great rattling is heard.)*

THE LADY

What's that?

A WHITE ANGEL

They've come!

THE LADY

Who have?

ANOTHER WHITE ANGEL

The Reds!
They're rattling their wings, but they've lost their heads!

THE FOUR WHITE ANGELS

>   *(Stroking their harps)*

Sing, sing, what shall we sing?
When the Reds are around, we can't think of a thing!
>   *(To an increased rattling,* FIVE RED ANGELS *enter with scarlet wings larger than the white wings of the Choir but with no heads.* ADAM *at the right with his drum,* EVE *at the left with her tambourine, beat time.)*

THE FIVE RED ANGELS

>   *(In lock-step)*

Left, right, left, right!
Make 'em go left when they want to go right!

THE FOUR WHITE ANGELS

Five of the Red Angels, four of the White—
And there's no Mussolini in heaven tonight!
>   (*The* RED ANGELS *draw the* WHITE ANGELS *into an interwoven jazz march, to the accompaniment of drum and tambourine, while the* LADY *stands aloof.*)

THE RED ANGELS

(One to each line)
Down with St. Peter and down with the Czar!
They're not the big punkins they think that they are.
Down with the harps and their heavenly humming!
Lenin is with us and Trotsky is coming.

THE WHITE ANGELS

(One to each line)
Here's to the Court and its heavenly vision!
We oppose the recall of a single decision.
Laugh at us, bully us, torture us, hate us—
We shall always oppose any change in our status.

THE RED AND WHITE ANGELS

(With alternating step and voice)
Left! Right! Left! Right!

THE WHITE ANGELS

The battle for heaven!

THE RED ANGELS

A hell of a fight!

A RED ANGEL

(Catching the LADY's *hand)*
She's surely a Red but not doing her share!
Magdalen, come and be true to your hair!

(During her struggle to be free, her hair comes off with the halo, leaving a frightened bob. Everything stops.)

ADAM

This isn't Mary Magdalen!

EVE

I told you so.

ADAM

(With a drum-beat)
You didn't.

EVE

(With a tambourine-shake)
I did.

ADAM

You didn't.

EVE

I did.

ADAM

(To the LADY*)*
What are you doing here?

THE LADY

I don't know.
But surely as handsome a man as you
Will understand me, whatever I do.

ADAM

Good woman—

EVE

Bad woman!

ADAM

Whichever you be,
We have counted a billion and seventy-three
Who have come here believing the one thing they needed
Was the Magdalen's halo.

THE LADY

She's lent it before?

ADAM

You girls are becoming a terrible bore.

EVE

(Picking up the halo and showing the LADY *something written on it)*
Can you read? Then observe what it says on the ticket.

THE LADY

(Reading)
"Good only if used by the person—"

ADAM

It's wicked,
To covet a neighbor's halo.
  (To the ANGELS*)*
Come!
Beat the suspension on Gabriel's drum!
  (A RED ANGEL *takes the drum.)*

THE LADY

(With a sudden firmness, trying to command the scene)
One moment, please! I have something to say, before you go on with your politics!

EVE

(Cramming the great angel-cake round the LADY's *neck)*
Here is a halo! One that sticks!

THE LADY

(On the edge of tears)
Wait till you see the book I write,
You'll be sorry for this night.
I shall call it, *Heaven, by One Who Knows*,
And there isn't a thing I shan't expose.
The world shall know you as you are!

ADAM

Beat the drum! Bring on the star!
> *(A RED ANGEL and a WHITE ANGEL bring, to drum-beats, a silver star with a bridle on its upper tip.)*

ADAM

(Handing her the halo)
Return it to Mary. How do you ride?

THE LADY

(Mounting the star with recovered dignity)
The only intelligent way. Astride.
> *(She writes on the inside cover of her express cheque-book.)*

EVE

What are you writing?

THE LADY

A note or two,
As noted writers always do.
> *(Writing and reading it aloud with withering inflection)*
"A witty paragraph on Eve's
Ill-fitting décolleté of leaves.
And one on Adam as a clown."

JUDAS

(Entering heaven from the right and crossing to her)
Have you enjoyed your tour through town?

It will cost you seven hundred francs.
> *(Taking her cheque-book from her dazed hand and tearing out cheques)*

The students offer you their thanks.

THE LADY

Students?

JUDAS

Meet them!
> *(As the* LADY *turns away)*

I insist.
Adam, the post-impressionist.
> *(When* ADAM *has shaken her limp hand)*

And an Eve, who was or is or will be
Two good feet ahead of Trilby.
> *(When* EVE *has shaken the other hand)*

Angels, forward!
> *(As the nine* ANGELS *step forward)*

The one who tore
The switches from your head—

THE LADY

No more!

ADAM

The Lady seems to be overcome.
Sound her a pick-me-up on the drum!
> *(One of the* ANGELS *beats a rolling salute.* EVE *gives the star and the* LADY *a shove down the ladder to the Boulevard.* JUDAS *follows. The curtains are drawn across heaven.)*

MARY

> *(Entering below)*

Did heaven suit you?

THE LADY

Never again.

MARY

You don't like angels?

THE LADY

Give me men.

JUDAS

Pardon us, Lady, we meant no harm.
We thought you would find a certain charm
In the students' impromptu masquerade—
But you look as if you'd been betrayed.

THE LADY

(With brisk hauteur)
Your intentions may have been of the best,
But practical jokes are a thing I detest.
The trouble is that you mistook me for an ordinary tourist
Or a lady-buyer or a manicurist;
But such dreadful Americans come abroad
Who have never heard of Cyril Maude
Or the Eiffel Tower or Brill or Keats
And even call refreshments "eats,"
That, though badly mistaken, you're forgiven
This opera buffet on heaven.
I am really a most distinguished person,
I have met the British King and Curzon;
And I have set aside all that
For a simple gown and a simple hat
And a very simple wish to go
On my own, incognito.
There must be people, besides the élite,
Whom it would be amusing to meet.
People who do things, people who think

Of more serious matters than food and drink.
I came to Paris to avoid
Conventional people. I should like to meet Freud,
People with minds, people with dash,
A notorious artist, or an Apache.

JUDAS

At whose expense?

THE LADY

My own. I never have to think about money.

JUDAS

Have you thirty pieces of silver?

THE LADY

That's not at all funny.
Bible jokes are the poorest of taste.
Put your arm around my waist.

JUDAS

Why?

THE LADY

Because it might lead to something. You know,
I have a frontier libido.

JUDAS

(Puzzled)
Do I follow you?

THE LADY

Follow me? Follow me where?
I'm tired. I want to sit down. I want a chair.

JUDAS

You might call to that artist. He has one under his arm.

THE LADY

Do you think that he—?

JUDAS

Try him and see.
It will do no harm.
    (JUDAS *and* MARY *watch the scene.*)

THE LADY

(Calling)
Artist, come here. I want to sit down. I'm tired.

AN ARTIST

(Entering)
This is no stool to be hired,
But consider it yours.

THE LADY

Open it.
    (Sitting)
Thank you.
    (Whispering)
Can't we be rid of these bores?

THE ARTIST

Judas and Mary? Not in a thousand years. We can put them behind us.
But wherever the sun may be, their shadows remain to remind us.

THE LADY

Why not put them in front of us, where they can't see?

THE ARTIST

As you like. They're nothing to me.

THE LADY

(To JUDAS and MARY)
Stop staring, please. It's time to reverse.

JUDAS

(To MARY)
Let's turn around. We might do worse.
> *(JUDAS and MARY face forward and stand so that they hide, respectively, the LADY and the ARTIST.)*

THE LADY

(Leaning with every speech out toward the ARTIST from behind JUDAS)
No one can see us now. This is splendid.

THE ARTIST

(Leaning with every speech out toward the LADY from behind MARY)
Be careful of that stool. I ought to have had it mended.

MARY

I hear it creaking. She may fall.

JUDAS

That wouldn't trouble her at all.

THE LADY

(Leaning out)
In Boston once I almost fainted—

THE ARTIST

(Leaning out)
Day before yesterday I painted—

THE LADY

When a librarian made love—

THE ARTIST

A Madonna with a dove—

THE LADY

Behind a book-case; wouldn't you?

THE ARTIST

In a robe of Prussian blue.

THE LADY

He talked too much.

THE ARTIST

It was hung too high,
So that everyone went by
Without noticing. But I can wait.

THE LADY

You can what? I can't. It's late.
I thought that in Paris things happened immediately.

THE ARTIST

You're wrong. Look at me.

THE LADY

I am looking at you,
What good does it do?

THE ARTIST

   (Excitedly)
By the way,
I painted yesterday
A really extraordinary canvas in the modern manner, I thought
   I'd try it,
And the thing is so brilliant that I have an idea you might like
   to buy it!

THE LADY

Even if I had the space for it, which I haven't, I wouldn't.

THE ARTIST

I ought to have known from your hat that you couldn't!
    (Crossing to JUDAS*)*
You promised me a patron, but who could make a sale
To this preposterous female?
    (The LADY's *indignation breaking the stool down, she falls with it.)*

THE ARTIST

    (Vehemently to the prostrate LADY*)*
Judas betrays us again and again,
He tries to make of us gentlemen.
We put on a spat and a white kid glove,
    (Tapping his heart)
And we bid farewell to the thing we love.
    (Tapping his trousers pocket)
He whispers to us where we're weak—

JUDAS

    (Lifting the edge of MARY's *skirt with his walking-stick)*
Notice the ankle! Isn't it chic?

THE ARTIST

    (Weakening)
And when for our art we would live and die,
He has a poser in reply.

MARY

    (Brightly)
I'll pose. I have to, for a living.
    (Taking the ARTIST's *arm)*
You'll find me useful—and forgiving.

JUDAS

(Smiling)
Another Magdalen, semi-nude.

THE LADY

(Still sitting, rubbing her wounded anatomy)
I might have done as much for him myself, if he hadn't been rude.
Once I am safely home again
In America where men are men,
I shall write a special chapter on the manners of the French,
Which have given my body a terrible wrench.
(Picking herself up and looking herself over)
But first there'll be new clothes to buy, and I'll need a new hat.

JUDAS

Go shopping. They always find comfort in that.

THE LADY

(Returning her head-dress to MARY)
Your halo.

MARY

It always comes back to me dirty.

THE LADY

(Haughtily to JUDAS, handing him a coin)
Your tip.

JUDAS

(Pocketing it)
But I thought it was going to be thirty.
Come, Mary, our little game is played.
They try to blame Judas, when they're self-betrayed.

THE LADY

I don't understand.

MARY

Oh yes, you do.
When the shoe fits, put on the shoe,
And don't attempt to wear, instead,
An ancient halo on a modern head.

THE LADY

I knew you weren't Mary, when you sprang
A while ago some modern slang—
But you spoke so beautifully before
About your poet.

MARY

It makes me sore,
The way these women always pull
Religion in to throw the bull.
Lady, Lady, give up your pose!
Wear rings on your fingers and bells on your toes!

THE LADY

I knew you were only a girl of the street,
Your trick was really not so neat:
But I said to myself, "We'll just pretend
To be taken in by our vulgar friend,
And that will afford us an excellent chance
To study the ways and means of France."

JUDAS

You're rather a muff at American bluff.
Study your own means. You've enough.

THE ARTIST

Leave her alone.

MARY

That's what she fears:
Being left alone, without any tears,

Without any feelings, without any shock.
> *(To the* LADY*)*

You can buy French pastry down the block.
> *(The* ARTIST *catches* MARY's *arm and goes gaily away with her.)*

THE LADY

> *(Calling through her hands toward the Height)*

Unicorn. A cable. You know what Paris heat is.
Come and take me home at once. Appendicitis.
> *(The upper curtains part, revealing the Height again. The* UNICORN, *putting down his newspaper, descends the ladder with the miniature steamer.)*

THE UNICORN

You'll feel much better when you've had a little air.

JUDAS

> *(Lifting the broken stool)*

How would this do for a steamer chair?
> *(Laughing,* JUDAS *lights a cigarette and strolls away. The* LADY *mounts the steamer behind the* UNICORN, *and they ascend the ladder. She sinks into her throne.)*

THE UNICORN

> *(Fanning her with his newspaper)*

Who reads a paper also serves.
Shall I send for a doctor?

THE LADY

No. It's nerves.
A little rest, and a body recovers.

THE UNICORN

How was Paris? Full of lovers?

THE LADY

(Ardently)
Full of students, charming creatures,
Nimble tongues and noble features.

THE UNICORN

It was said long since by somebody like Joel Chandler Harris,
That when an American goes to heaven, he finds himself in Paris.

THE LADY

Paris really was a riot.
But what I need now is a little quiet.

THE UNICORN

(Ringing the gong)
What ho, a little quiet!
> *(The eight* SERVANTS *enter and bow forward. When one of them has covered the gong with a large worsted motto, "A Little Quiet," they all leave on tiptoe.)*

THE LADY

Unicorn, you are the only one whom I can ever tell.
Paris wasn't heaven.
(Sobbing)
It was hell.

CURTAIN

ACT II

(Strewn around the LADY, *seated on her throne, are many books concerning China. She throws a very large book to the floor. It wakes the* UNICORN, *who has been dozing in one of his chairs.)*

THE UNICORN

(Striking the gong)
More books on China!
(Servants enter with more.)

THE LADY

I've read enough.
I'm full to bursting with this travel-stuff.

THE UNICORN

Would you rather stay at home than go?

THE LADY

Buy me a diamond kimono.
I want to see what I can do,
As the darky put it, "to unscrew
The inscrutable." Bid all the servants hurry
And pack me a ton of cake,—so I shan't have to live on curry.

THE UNICORN

Not curry, Lady.

THE LADY

Well, chop suey.
Whatever they eat, it's much too gooey.
Therefore I intend to take

A private supply of American cake.
And I want some whiskey and some gin
To squander on a Mandarin.
Chinese, I understand, are slow.

    THE UNICORN

    (*Yawning and striking the gong*)
Whiskey and gin and cake, what ho!
    (*Darkness.*)
    (*An interlude of Chinese music.*)
    Light reveals, in China, a tea-table of teak-wood and marble, with a chair on either side of it of the same materials. In one of them sits a young MANDARIN, *dressed in the ancient official robes. He is sheltering his nose with a yellow silk handkerchief. One of the* LADY'S SERVANTS *enters from the side and, delivering the parchment message, leaves again. The* MANDARIN *reads it, gravely nodding, while two others of her* SERVANTS *bring in and leave behind them a ton of cake and a hamper of bottles. The* UNICORN *unfolds the ladder leading down from the Height into China, then returns to his newspaper and is hidden by the closing of the upper curtains.*)

    THE LADY

    (*Descending the ladder in smart travelling costume of gold*)
So this is China. Why do you hold your nose?

    THE MANDARIN

Because of the ancestral wind that blows.
I like my ancestors in their books,—not in my nostrils, unless
    I must.
There is too much camel-dung mixed with their dust.
But who can be dignified against the wind?

    THE LADY

    (*Sitting in the other chair*)
A drunkard can—or a woman who has sinned.

THE MANDARIN

(Lowering the handkerchief)
You have said the very mouthful I have tasted.
(He spits.)

THE LADY

(Wisely)
And except for wine and sin, how life is wasted!

THE MANDARIN

I have watched your Western folk forever coming,
Asses with blinders made of perfect plumbing.
And yet I compliment you on your way
Of breathing bits of wisdom when you bray.

THE LADY

What do you mean by that? It doesn't sound—

THE MANDARIN

Your last remark, for instance. I have found
That a drunken man leans always with the wind.
And, as you say, a woman who has sinned
Lightly permits the everlasting dust
To penetrate the crevice of her bust.
Lean with the wind. Accept the universe.
Allow the desert-sand to intersperse
Its grains. Take in your teeth
Ironic relish of the air you breathe.
O Laotzu, listen to this word of hers!
Despite commercial travellers,
Theirs is a country simpler than it seems.
Not what they say but what they do redeems
Vulgarity. Their moneymaking melts like vapour in a glass of wine.
Their virtue is a fragile columbine,

Nodding to vice. I use the terms they use,
Terms that confuse
Brains more accustomed to realities.

THE LADY

(Removing the outer garment from her diamond kimono)
Mandarin, look at me, look at me, please!

THE MANDARIN

Why should I look at you?

THE LADY

To see
If you might not take an interest in me.

THE MANDARIN

At what percent?

THE LADY

(Coyly lifting a bottle from the hamper)
I am the dividends—after a cocktail.

THE MANDARIN

Oh, my native friends,
She's not the cocktail, she's the dividends!

THE LADY

You twist my words.

THE MANDARIN

The lemon-peel, my dear.

THE LADY

You know our customs?

THE MANDARIN

Very well, I fear.
You load your missionaries in your guns,
And in your motor-cars you breed your sons.
And now your sons are teaching mine
That the sign of the cross is a dollar sign.

THE LADY

Have you, by any chance, a cocktail-shaker?

THE MANDARIN

I am an expert as an undertaker.
You know our custom. In the midst of life,
We are in death. We decorate the knife
With which to stab ourselves. We buy
The very box in which our bones prefer to lie.
Shall I send for mine, to show to you?

THE LADY

(With a smile)
A Chinese coffin big enough for two?
I guess I'm game.

THE MANDARIN

(Clapping his hands, with a smile)
I'm sure you are.
(To the ivory-faced SERVANT *who enters)*
Bring me the Shaker of the Purple Star,
Two naked grapes, a few pomegranate-seeds,
The evening-dew from seven river-reeds,
Eleven petals of the passion-flower,—
And a bottle of Gordon Gin.
(As the SERVANT *takes it from the* LADY's *offering hand)*
And bring me from the tower,
Solemnly I ask it,
My own, my personal, my chosen casket.

THE LADY

(To her audience)
This is experience, upon my word!
Has any one of you ever heard
Of a courtship in a coffin?
> *(Two* SERVANTS *bring a large, boat-like coffin, decorated with bright dragons, and go out again.)*

THE MANDARIN

Do you approve of it?

THE LADY

I'll say I do!

THE MANDARIN

Then try it.

THE LADY

Coming with me?

THE MANDARIN

After you.
> *(When they have climbed into the coffin and sit side by side)*

Dragons can hiss,
When we abuse their dignity like this.

THE LADY

We're naughty, aren't we!

THE MANDARIN

What do your silly terms
Amount to on this journey among worms?

THE LADY

Don't be so realistic!

THE MANDARIN

Very well. We'll give them wings and claws
And call them dragons.

THE LADY

(Leaning toward the ton of cake and breaking off a piece)
Can't you be cheerful? Come on, Santa Claus,
Summon your slaves
To bring me presents.

THE MANDARIN

(Calling to SERVANTS *outside)*
Open up the graves!
We shall see what gifts have lasted.

THE LADY

Why so creepy?
(Leaning on his shoulder and nibbling her cake)
Something has to happen, I'm growing sleepy.

THE MANDARIN

But what can happen when you're leaning on
The peaked shoulder of a skeleton?
Surely there's nothing very beautiful
Within the shadowy sockets of a skull—
(As SERVANTS *arrive and leave behind the cups and the
Shaker of the Purple Star)*
But a cocktail proves that we're still alive.
Shall I serve you one?

THE LADY

Or two.

THE MANDARIN

Or five.

THE LADY

Will you have some cake?

THE MANDARIN

(Shaking his head)
Why not the moon?
It's so much larger than a macaroon!

THE LADY

Why do you shake your head?

THE MANDARIN

Because you ache
In all your centers from excess of cake.
  (He pours the liquor into seven cups.)

THE LADY

Are you filling seven cups at once?

THE MANDARIN

I am.
It makes a more diverting diagram.

THE LADY

But that's not customary.

THE MANDARIN

Sorry.
I need all seven to tell a story.
  (He lifts a cup.)
With this, you see me as a little child
Who drinks his mother's milk and finds it mild.
  (He drains the cup and lifts another.)
With this, I am a boy, tasting the curl—

THE LADY

But Chinese hair is straight!

THE MANDARIN

Of a little girl.
   (He drains the second.)
With this, I am a youth, kissing a throat.
   (He drains the third and kisses her throat.)
With this, a breast.
   (The fourth, and kisses her breast.)
With this, I dote
On mistresses.
   (The fifth, and puts his arm around her.)
With this I create a need.
   (The sixth, and kisses her ear.)
With this, I yawn and fall asleep.
   (He drains the seventh cup and lies down in the coffin, away from her.)

THE LADY

   (Rising)
Indeed!
   (The MANDARIN'S SERVANTS enter.)

A SERVANT

We shall bury his body under the ancient moon.

THE LADY

What do you mean? He's asleep! He'll wake up soon.

THE SERVANT

It's all the same. His father's field will do.

THE OTHER SERVANT

   (Taking a handle of the coffin)
Shall we bury both of them? The lady too?

THE LADY

Be careful now! You don't know what this means!
I'll cable Washington! They'll send marines!
You put this coffin down and let me out!
    (Stepping out of it)
Then do whatever you want to with that lout!
The trouble with me is I'm hungry. For God's sake,
Can't any one of you fetch me a piece of cake?
    (Calling)
The ladder, Unicorn, the ladder, quick!
    (The UNICORN, *between parting curtains, lets down the ladder.)*

THE UNICORN

    (As she reaches the top)
Have you found experience?

THE LADY

You make me sick!

THE UNICORN

Then we must make you well again.
Shall it be medicine? Or men?
    (The LADY *returns to her throne.)*

THE MANDARIN

    (Stepping out of the coffin and brushing crumbs from his coat)
Imagine me dying before I wake
And lying for years in a box of cake.
Order me another coffin.
This one is haunted
By too many things the lady wanted.

THE LADY

(Vaguely)
A piece of cake.
(As the CAKE-SERVANT *serves her)*
And who are you?

THE CAKE-SERVANT

Cake-Servant, Madam.

THE LADY

(Noticing him)
How do you do!

CURTAIN

ACT III

(The LADY *and the* UNICORN *are discovered again on the Height, he at first asleep over his paper.)*

THE LADY

(Taking his paper and striking him awake)
Unicorn, be a phœnix for once!
Arise from your ashes,
Put fire into that dead old heart of yours!
You cannot play music on a horn that is closed at both ends.
Make, then, of your horn a flaming beak,
Tip your tongue with jets from the jungle
To lighten the Jews and the Gentiles! . . .
If you are to advise me any longer,
Do not whisper to me of civilizations
And their cunning use of me,
But shout around me nations
Of naked ebony!
Show me the moon pierced by their spears!
Make me drunk with the smell of moony blood!
I am sick of civilization. Put gigantic drums into my ears!
Cake me with mud!

THE UNICORN

(Amazed)
What has done this
To your dumbness?
I never knew you'd a thought
To your name, I confess it,
Much less a way to express it.

THE LADY

It has always been here inside me, but I was taught
To repress it.
I have had to go through my paces,
To want to see white teeth in black faces.

THE UNICORN

(Sinister)
So that is what you have wanted!
The very desire of it has given you words.
I shall find you a jungle haunted
With obscene birds,
With reptiles to lash you and with black ooze
To embrace you the way you choose!
You shall give your breath
To a constrictor! And when you are dead,
A vulture will come with a thin varicose head!

THE LADY

Who asked you to order me death?
And your vultures! Don't be absurd!
I want a strong-smelling, black-bodied panther,
Not a foul-smelling, bald-headed bird!

THE UNICORN

(In a released frenzy)
Oh, to see you feel your soft flesh torn with a rush
Of horny finger-nails and your throat purple from the push
Of great thumbs!
(Striking the gong)
Start the drums!
(Continuing to the deep pulse of drum-beats)
You have betrayed me with your wish to be taken.
I am shaken
With anger against you. Dismiss me, of course,

It had to come sooner or later.
I am a good servant, but oh, what a hater!
If I might only see the hoofs of a wild horse
Trampling your face and hear your cries
And watch the vulture plucking out your eyes
And laugh at your silly hands trying to hold back your bowels
From a jackal's jowls!

THE LADY

You are dismissed.

THE UNICORN

I can see you being kissed
By an alligator. I hope it hurts!

THE LADY

You are mad!

THE UNICORN

So are you.

THE LADY

(With a sob)
And yet what shall I do,
If you leave me? I shall never know what I'm about.
Who will carry out
My orders? You are the only one of them all who can bake
Cake!

THE UNICORN
(Sullen)
Lady, your money has made me too fat.
I need to reduce now, with the proletariat.

THE LADY

O Unicorn, I can give you less pay!

THE UNICORN

Very well, I shall stay.

THE LADY

That was almost a bungle.
And who
But you
Could find me a jungle?

THE UNICORN

So you'll risk being hurt?

THE LADY

(In an ecstasy)
I have always been aching to wear a grass skirt!
   (Darkness)
   (Negro music)
   *(Light reveals in an African jungle a black savage, naked
   but for a loin-cloth made of fig-leaves and one ostrich
   feather, and a pyramidal head-dress of monkey-skulls.
   He carries a great bloody club.)*

THE NEGRO

I have eaten the moons, I have eaten the suns!
One a penny, two a penny, hot cross buns!

THE LADY

   *(Coming between the closed curtains and descending the
   ladder, proud of her grass-skirt)*
At last!

THE NEGRO

   (Licking his lips)
Breakfast!

THE LADY

Do you mean that your tribe is cannibal?

THE NEGRO

It was until I ate them all.
There were plenty of people a while ago,
But now there's nobody left I know.
I ate this morning at half past three
A friend who disagreed with me.
Don't worry. I'm not hungry yet.
Perhaps I'll keep you for a pet.

THE LADY

That would be delightful. I've always been the one
To keep the pets. And the pets have all the fun.
But do people really taste good?

THE NEGRO

Only proper kind of food—
    (*With increased rhythm*)
Cooked on hot stones, covered with leaves,
Tenderer than bush-pigs, better than beeves!
Cattle eat grass, chickens eat corn,
But men eat men, sure as you're born.
Some like 'em lean, but I like 'em fat.
Where have you been that you don't know that?

THE LADY

Ask me where I haven't been.

THE NEGRO

Is that the reason you're so thin?

THE LADY

Then you won't eat me!

THE NEGRO

(Picking up a large black-headed pin and a palette)
Not for a while.
But I got to see to it that you dress in style.

THE LADY

What in the world are you going to do?

THE NEGRO

The very latest in tattoo!
   *(Beginning with a Charleston step to jazz the pin into the
   colours and then, on final accents, into the* LADY's *back)*
Dip it in the dark one, dip it in the light one,
Dip it in the black one, dip it in the white one,
Dip it in, dip it in, dip it in, dip—
Dip it in the débutante to carry on the hip.

THE LADY

(Hypnotized, joining him in jazz)
Hurts like sin, hurts like sin!

THE NEGRO

Dip it, dip it, dip it, dip it, dip it, dip it, *in!*

THE LADY

Never had a prejudice, never gave a rip—

THE NEGRO

Dip it in, dip it in, dip it in, *dip!*

THE LADY

Colour isn't anything, never should have been—

THE NEGRO

Dip it, dip it, dip, dip, dip it, dip it, *in!*

THE LADY

Went to Louisiana, taken on a trip—

THE NEGRO

Dip it in, dip it in, dip it in, *dip!*

THE LADY

Saw a lot o' niggers, told by my kin—

THE NEGRO

Dip, dip, dip it, dip, dip it, dip it, *in!*

THE LADY

Only way to treat 'em, treat 'em with a whip—

THE NEGRO

Only way to treat 'em, treat 'em to a nip—

THE LADY

Tell me what the pattern is you're painting with a pin!

THE NEGRO

Nip, nip, nip, nip, nip o', nip o' gin!

THE LADY

Tell me what you're doing, poking at my hip!

THE NEGRO

Every time I poke at you, I poke a poker-chip.
   (*He twirls her about, revealing on her back a wild pattern of red, white and blue poker-chips.*)

THE LADY

   (*Motionless but still hypnotized*)
Make me as beautiful as you are.
I am sure that your breasts are set with sapphires
And your navel with a moonstone.

THE NEGRO

No, they're not. You can see that they're not.

THE LADY

That has nothing to do with it.

THE NEGRO

Nothing to do with what? What are you giving us?

THE LADY

(*Exultant*)
Life. Its inner meaning!

THE NEGRO

But my breasts are not set with anything
And my navel's just a navel. Please, not a moonstone!
If you must be fancy, for heaven's sake—

THE LADY

(*With an inspiration*)
A black pearl on a devil-cake!

THE NEGRO

Now you're talking! That's the i!
But would they understand it, at home in Hawaii?

THE LADY

I'm not from Hawaii.

THE NEGRO

What do you mean?
Aren't you the hula-hula queen?

THE LADY

Because of the skirt that I have on?
I only wore the thing for fun.
I'm from New York.

THE NEGRO

(Excited)

That's my town too!

THE LADY

Your town?

THE NEGRO

My town.

THE LADY

Your town?

THE NEGRO

Sho—
I'm from Harlem. That's my town.

THE LADY

But what are you doing with a great big crown?

THE NEGRO

Hell, Lady, I've been down here two months now, with nothin'
    to dress in but sweat,
And it isn't worth it, not on your life, for the little bit I get.
At first it was funny, loafin' around, it used to make me grin;
But now I hate it, honest to God, I hate the job like sin.

THE LADY

The feather, the skulls, the bloody knob!
Is this another put-up job?
Are you a student?

THE NEGRO

I'm a fool.
And what are you doing out of school?
I thought you'd been added to the show—

And I sure was glad to see you, bo,
For I've been in the damnedest dumps
Since the camera-fellow came down with the mumps.
Nothing to do!

THE LADY

The camera-fellow?

THE NEGRO

He ought to be working, but he's yellow.

THE LADY

Working at what?

THE NEGRO

At shooting the vamp.

THE LADY

(Outraged)
Is this a moving-picture camp?

THE NEGRO

That's what it is, but don't blame me.

THE LADY

You black impostor!

THE NEGRO

There, you see?
We always get it, because we're black.
But you're part coloured. Look at your back.

THE LADY

Won't come off?

THE NEGRO

In for good.

THE LADY

Oh, I shall never be understood!
Can't go to dances any more.

THE NEGRO

That would depend on what you wore.
I took great care to place those chips
Just a little bit over the hips.

THE LADY

You brute!

THE NEGRO

You don't mean that at all.
You thought I was great as a cannibal,
But you didn't like to be surprised
And find that I was civilized.
What were you looking for anyway?

THE LADY

You be careful what you say,
You low-down nigger!

THE NEGRO

There, you see?

THE LADY

Don't you roll your eyes at me!

THE NEGRO

If I can't roll my eyes, what can I do?
Might as well sing for a minute or two.
    (Singing)
"Swing low, sweet chariot,
Coming for to carry me home,
Swing low, sweet chariot, coming for to carry me home."

(In answer to his appeal, there descends beside him a workman's rope-seat hung from a pulley.)

THE LADY

Is this a part of the movie act?

THE NEGRO

No, Lady, this is a actual fact,
"Coming for to carry me home."
Feeling homesick? Want to go?

THE LADY

(Superbly)
Not if the chariot isn't Jim Crow.
If a man were around you wouldn't presume.

THE NEGRO

(Gently)
I'm sorry, Lady, but there isn't much room.

THE LADY

With a nigger? Never.

THE NEGRO

Very well.
(He pulls a loose halyard, which rings a siren-whistle in the chariot.)

THE LADY

(Startled)
You ought to be lynched for ringing that bell!

THE NEGRO

(Climbing into the seat)
I had to, to start it.

THE LADY

Up on your feet!
Instantly! I wish that seat!

THE NEGRO

(Plaintive)
It's my own chariot.

THE LADY

One of your race?
This is a national disgrace.

THE NEGRO

(Praying)
What shall I do, Lord, what shall I do?

GOD'S VOICE

(From above)
Stay put.

THE NEGRO

Praise God! Hallelu!

THE LADY

If I ever get you into court,
You'll pay for this, you will!

GOD'S VOICE

What port?

THE NEGRO

(His face uplifted)
I hear you! Take me to Harlem, Lord!

THE LADY

(Desperate)
He's off to Harlem!

GOD'S VOICE

All aboard!
(The chariot begins to rise, with a rope hanging from it.)

THE NEGRO

Chariot swings, chariot swings!
When I get to Harlem, going to put on my things!
Chariot swings, chariot swings—

THE LADY

(Seizing the rope)
He'll never notice, and no one'll know me,
I'll be just a grass-skirt to the people below me.
I'm really heroic, I'm not on the seat,
I'll be home pretty soon, there'll be something to eat.
(She gives a shrill cry as the chariot lifts. The NEGRO, *still chanting, pulls the siren, which continues its sound, while a camera-man enters just in time to take a movie of the dangling and disappearing* LADY.*)*

CURTAIN

ACT IV

(The risen curtain reveals the LADY *and the* UNICORN *at home on the Height.)*

THE UNICORN

It is the order of the day.

THE LADY

What is?

THE UNICORN

Whatever you order is the order of the day.
After the hardness of your recent experiences,
Perhaps you would like mush. Shall it be mush?

THE LADY

(With great dignity)
It shall be locusts and wild honey.

THE UNICORN

(Bowing)
Wild honey, yes.
But I have never known, my Lady,
Whether locusts meant the insect or the tree.
If you will tell me which is uppermost in your appetite—

THE LADY

Order me both.

THE UNICORN

Why both?

THE LADY

To make sure of its being locusts.

THE UNICORN

(Striking the gong)
What ho, wild honey! What ho, locusts!
(To the eight entering SERVANTS)
Half of you are to bring wild honey—

A SERVANT

Where from?

THE UNICORN

Wild bees.

THE SERVANT

Aren't all bees wild?

THE UNICORN

And half of you locusts.

A SECOND SERVANT

Locusts?

THE UNICORN

Half of the half of you are to bring insects
And the other half of the half of you trees.

THE SECOND SERVANT

How are we to tell locusts from other trees?

THE UNICORN

Encyclopaedia Britannica.

A THIRD SERVANT

But the volume with the L's in it is lost.

THE LADY

Buy two volumes with the L's in them,
While you are about it, buy three.
And then we shall have as many locusts as we need.

THE UNICORN

One volume will be enough, my Lady.

THE LADY

(Sternly)
One volume will not be enough.
I intend to eat locusts and wild honey
All the rest of my life.

THE UNICORN

Why in the world this permanent change of diet?

THE LADY

It is not to be in the world any longer
But out of the world.
I have had enough chow mein, enough Bar le Duc,
I have had too many cocktails and cocoanuts!
In other words, I have profited by my experiences.

THE UNICORN

Your experiences were supposed to be not of the stomach
But of the heart and head.

THE LADY

They have turned my stomach.

THE UNICORN

To locusts and wild honey?

THE LADY

I want wisdom and peace,
Not the wisdom of Paris nor the peace of Peking,
Nor the restlessness of grass-skirts,
But the peace that passeth understanding
Except in India.
I shall prepare my body with light foods,
To receive a Swami.

THE UNICORN

But locusts and wild honey
Are a menu of the Near East, not of the Far East.

THE LADY

As I remember my geography, Unicorn,
I shall have to be passing through the Near East
On my way to the Far East.
One East at a time will be all that I can manage.

THE UNICORN

(*To the* SERVANTS)
This, then, is the order of the day.
The half of the half of you who are to bring insects
Are to join the half of the half of you who are to bring trees,
And the other half of you who are to bring honey
Are to join both the half of the other half of you who are to
    bring insects
And the other half of the other half of you who are to bring trees;
For on the one tree are to be found at the same time
The wildest honey and the most luscious insects;
And at the same time with the same time,
The tree is itself a locust. And there you are.
I am valuable to you, my Lady.
This is a great saving not only of the same time but of the same
    space.

This is what is known as system,
Co-ordination, scientific management.

THE LADY

Then manage me something else.
I intend in India to be a beggar.
If I am to be a beggar, I must have a bowl.
And it must be a beautiful bowl,
A bowl of jade, a cup of rhinoceros-horn,
No, not a bowl of jade, two bowls of jade,
No, make it three, three bowls of jade
And three cups of rhinoceros-horn,
One of green jade, one of white jade, and one of yellow jade,
A young rhinoceros, a middle-aged rhinoceros, and an old
    rhinoceros,
And then I shall have enough bowls to be a beggar.
For if they offer me more food than I can eat on a given day,
I shall have something laid aside to eat on an ungiven day.

THE UNICORN

You will be taking to the East a new wisdom.

THE LADY

(Brightening)
You think so?

THE UNICORN

You will be taking them efficiency.
And soon there will be factories all over India
For the making of bowls and cups.

THE LADY

Bowls of jade and cups of rhinoceros-horn!

THE UNICORN

And some of them will be of celluloid.

THE LADY

Oh, not of celluloid!
I couldn't bear to be the introducer
Of anything so cheap as celluloid.

THE UNICORN

But it will not be so cheap over there, my Lady.
You will control the factories that make it,
There will be a duty against importing it,
Gandhi himself will be advocating native celluloid.
Soon they will be manufacturing whole altars of celluloid,
And their happiness in celluloid will make you rich.

THE LADY

I can be rich there and still be a beggar?

THE UNICORN

To be a successful beggar, you have to be rich.

THE LADY

There must be beauty about me when I beg.
I think I should like to do it in the Taj Mahal.

THE UNICORN

You shall do it in the Taj Mahal.

THE LADY

Can it be arranged?

THE UNICORN

Anything can be arranged, my Lady,
With the British Empire.

THE LADY

What are the servants waiting for?

THE UNICORN

To see what more you need, to be a beggar.

THE LADY

I think I shall need a veil, to be a beggar.
Don't women in India, all of them, wear veils?
   (To the SERVANTS*)*
Bring me three hundred and sixty-five white veils,
No, not white veils, coloured veils,
Of three hundred and sixty-five different colours,
And that will be all for today.
Reverse.

THE UNICORN

You are to reverse, from now on, of your own accord.
   (The SERVANTS *bow backwards and leave on their errands.)*

THE UNICORN

I am wondering something, Lady.

THE LADY

What are you wondering?

THE UNICORN

If you might not find peace and wisdom nearer home.

THE LADY

What would the neighbors say?

THE UNICORN

We might ask them.

THE LADY

But I can't bear to think of their thinking that I think
My previous way of thinking not the way to think.
And besides, how can they be worth asking, when they're not
   worth knowing?

THE UNICORN

Then why should you care what they say?

THE LADY

Because words are more important than people.
> (*The* SERVANTS *enter excitedly with branches, insects, and wild honey.*)

A SERVANT

We found a locust-tree growing in our own court-yard!

A SECOND SERVANT

Covered with bees!

A THIRD SERVANT

And with locusts!

THE LADY

The bowls and the cups?

A FOURTH SERVANT

The Museum offers you its jades.

A FIFTH SERVANT

And the Zoo its rhinoceros.

THE LADY

And I must take a present for a Swami.
What shall it be?

THE UNICORN

A pair of sandals?

THE LADY

No. I am thinking for myself today.
It shall be a hair-shirt, made of my own hair,

The hair that was bobbed off me.
Look in the second bureau-drawer of the seventh bedroom
And find my prettiest undervest of lavender.
Let it be lined deliciously with my own hair,
And I shall take it as a present to a Swami
To wear on Sundays.
He shall wear whatever shirt he like on the other days of the
    week,
But this one on Sundays.

THE UNICORN

Sunday is not Sunday over there.

THE LADY

But I shall be there, and I know when it's Sunday.
And if one Swami refuses to wear it on Sunday,
I shall give it to some other Swami.
There are plenty of Swamis, aren't there?

THE UNICORN

I know of one Swami in India, my Lady.
And if one Swami should not be enough,
Cable at once and we shall send you
Dozens of Swamis from America.

THE LADY

If there are Swamis in America,
Why must I leave?

THE UNICORN

Because to know a Swami
You must be a beggar.
Imagine begging on Fifth Avenue.

THE LADY

Proceed with the arrangements.
Charter me a steamer.

Bring lapidaries for the bowls
And hire, for the rhinoceros-horn,
A chiropodist or whatever you call him.
Pick me a milliner from Fifth Avenue with all her veilings,
Give her the bridal suite.
I shall go steerage and prepare to be simple.
Bring enough ice for the honey, enough locusts for the leaves
And enough leaves for the locusts.
And I must carry in one hand—for the colour—
A pomegranate.

THE UNICORN

(Striking the gong)
What ho, a pomegranate!
   (A SERVANT *serves her a pomegranate from a fruit-dish.)*

THE LADY

And in the other hand—?

THE UNICORN

Shall it be a lotus?

THE LADY

No, not a lotus.
Are Swamis clean?

THE UNICORN

Not always.

THE LADY

In the other hand I shall carry—
Bring it at once—a cake of soap.
   (A SERVANT *serves her from a soap dish a cake of lavender soap.)*
   (The LADY, *in beautiful simplicity, descends from her Height, bearing in one hand the pomegranate, in the other*

the cake of soap. The UNICORN follows her and at the foot of
the ladder is given by a breathless SERVANT the lavender
undervest and the long hair. They attend the LADY in
procession, the SERVANTS with locusts and wild honey being
joined by other SERVANTS with bowls of jade, cups of
rhinoceros-horn, and veils of many colours. They pass out
to the left on the journey toward a SWAMI.)
(Darkness.)
(Music of India.)
(To a tinkling of temple-bells and the windy hum of a
tamboura, the veiled LADY and her procession, lacking only
the UNICORN, approach in India an elderly, long-haired
SWAMI, one half of whose beard is black and the other half
white. He sits cross-legged with a bowl before him. The
LADY prostrates herself toward him. The SERVANTS one after
another deposit behind her the various articles she has
brought. The SWAMI, at first indifferent to the interrupters of
his meditation, notes with growing interest the arrival of
goods and finally prostrates himself toward the LADY, so that
their backs make the very human arch of mutual
admiration. The SERVANTS pause a moment, grinning at the
strange sight; and the last one to leave cannot resist
speaking just one word.)

THE SERVANT

Reverse!
  (The LADY instantly turns about on all fours, facing away
  from the SWAMI.)

  THE SWAMI

Where are you going?

  THE LADY

I don't know.
  (As a comely young DISCIPLE, carrying a bowl, enters
  unnoticed behind them)

I think I'm going East.
Oughtn't we to face Mecca before we begin?

THE SWAMI

Begin what?

THE LADY

I don't know.
I want you to tell me.

THE SWAMI

I can tell you first,
We are on a road that has neither beginning nor ending;
And I can tell you second,
Wherever we face, we face holiness.

THE LADY

But I can think of things—

THE DISCIPLE

To face Mecca from here, you would have to face west.

THE LADY

(Turning toward the DISCIPLE *and rising, eagerly)*
Are you a beggar?

THE DISCIPLE

If you wish to call me what I am not.

THE LADY

But your bowl?

THE DISCIPLE

We save people from thinking too little and from eating too
 much.
Therefore they beg us to eat. It is they who are the beggars.

THE LADY

Are you hungry now?

THE SWAMI

(Still on all fours)
We have no desires.

THE LADY

(Still to the DISCIPLE, her hand on his arm)
But if I beg you to be hungry? I have wild honey.

THE DISCIPLE

(Moving away from her)
Give it to the Master. I am only the Disciple.

THE LADY

I have enough for you both.
This for you.
   (Quickly placing in the SWAMI's bowl a large insect)
And this for you.
   (Tenderly placing a comb of honey in the DISCIPLE's bowl)

THE SWAMI

(Looking down his beard into the bowl)
What little I had the locust has consumed in one gulp.

THE DISCIPLE

Then give the locust my honeycomb. For he is the hungry one.
And to think that the hungry one might have been eaten!
   (To the LADY)
Has no one taught you that the souls of our ancestors may be
   doing penance in locusts?
If the Master had been blind, he might have eaten his
   grandmother.

THE LADY

But if, as the Master says, all places are holy,
Why shouldn't the locust do penance in the stomach?

THE SWAMI

(Solemnly)
The intestines are too long a journey for the soul.

THE LADY

I knew there was some reason why I didn't like them,
Locusts, I mean. I brought the wrong kind.
But I have brought the right kind too, for a salad.
Oh dear, I forgot to bring any Tarragon vinegar!
Or perhaps the locust is somebody's family tree?
It might be better to use the branches for shade.
I freckle. We'd better use them for shade.

THE SWAMI

(Turning, finally, from his posture)
Have you never learned that sun and shade are one,
That day and night are growing from God's face
Like the black and white commingled in my beard?

THE LADY

(To the DISCIPLE)
Would your beard, if it grew,
Grow day and night like his?

THE DISCIPLE

(Gravely)
All beards are growing day and night.
    (He shelters the SWAMI with locust boughs.)

THE LADY

Why are you putting the branches over him,
And none over you and me?

THE DISCIPLE

Because he will not notice the difference.
If I put them over you, you would notice the difference.

THE LADY

(Uneasy in the heat)
I wish them over me.

THE SWAMI

You wish to be comfortable.

THE LADY

I only wish what you are wishing.

THE SWAMI

You should wish nothing.

THE LADY

Not wisdom and peace?

THE SWAMI

Wisdom cannot be used for our own purposes,
Nor peace for a garment against the sun.
   (The DISCIPLE *removes his upper garment, revealing a fine young body.)*

THE LADY

(Eagerly)
Shall I remove mine?

THE DISCIPLE

No, Master. Remember what happened last time!

THE SWAMI

It might be as well to test you.

THE DISCIPLE

Master, no!

THE LADY

What happened?

THE DISCIPLE

I was gone nine days and nine nights;
And during my absence the dogs ate two of his toes.

THE SWAMI

Without my noticing the difference.

THE LADY

To think of their going to the dogs!

THE SWAMI

I desire that you leave us . . .
No, I desire nothing.
    (*He removes his upper garment, revealing a thin old body. The* DISCIPLE *turns his back on the* LADY, *places his bowl before him and sits, cross-legged. The* LADY *picks up two bowls of jade and two cups of rhinoceros-horn and sits on the other side of the* DISCIPLE *where he can see her.*)

THE LADY

I'm going to be quiet now. I'm going to beg.
May I remove—?

THE DISCIPLE

No.

THE LADY

My veil?

THE SWAMI

I do not hear you.

THE LADY

(Removing her veil and sighing)
So much more peaceful!
Do I look peaceful?

THE DISCIPLE

I do not see you.

THE LADY

(Suiting the action to the rapid words)
While you are not hearing and not seeing,
I shall take for myself your ordinary bowls
And give to each of you, with my compliments,
A bowl of jade and a cup of rhinoceros-horn
Which I have had copied from museum pieces in Peking,
Where the beggars are different from the beggars here,
Impostors mostly, none of them saints like you—
In Nanking by the temple-gate, a woman
Pounding her own bosom black and blue,
For no reason at all except that her great-great-grandmother
Had probably pounded—

THE SWAMI

We have forgotten you.

THE LADY

Had pounded a bosom blowing now as dust
Over the roofs and into people's teeth,
As a Mandarin said to me once, making love to me in a coffin.
  (She pauses as PASSERS-BY *enter and, leaving coins and food
  in the bowls of the holy men but none in hers, go their way.)*

THE LADY

I wonder why people forget the beauty of holiness,
Like an artist I knew in Paris once, who only thought of himself
And painted the most awful daubs I ever saw,

Except that I didn't see them, wouldn't give him the satisfaction,
   and why should I,
When he didn't have a thing in his mind except animal pleasures
And never once in his life could have meditated
As we are meditating now.
   (*Other* PASSERS-BY *cross and ignore the* LADY *in favour of the holy men.*)

THE LADY

I don't believe they know that I'm a beggar.
They think that I'm just sitting here.
The pomegranate—
   (*Crossing and picking it up*)
As a symbol of hunger.
And the cake of soap, as a symbol of purity.
   (*Resuming her position, pomegranate in one hand, cake of soap in the other, crossing her legs this time*)
So many mosquitoes! How do you manage it?
It might be better if I sang a song.
If only I had learned a Hindu song!
What sort of songs do Hindu beggars sing?
O yes, I know. "Less—" That's not the pitch.
   (*Trying another pitch and singing as the first group of* PASSERS-BY *returns*)
"Less than the dust beneath thy chariot wheel—"
   (*She cannot remember more of the song and therefore repeats the first line several times, while the* PASSERS-BY *give the* LADY *only a smile of mingled amazement and amusement and go their way.*)

THE LADY

I know what the trouble is. Too many clothes.

THE DISCIPLE

O Master, what shall I do if she—?

THE SWAMI

Meditate!
> (She removes an upper garment, then suddenly leaps to her feet.)

THE LADY

I'm sitting on an ant-hill! Oh, I'm bitten!
Stop meditating for a minute, please!
I think I'm going to faint. I know I am!
> (She crosses to the DISCIPLE and faints beside him with her head on his shoulder, which hardens like rock.)

THE SWAMI

She's moving. Meditate.

THE DISCIPLE

I'm trying to.

THE LADY

> (Opening an eye)

Even a saint might be a gentleman.

THE DISCIPLE

I do not feel you.

THE LADY

> (Pinching him)

Do you feel me now?

THE DISCIPLE

O Master, succour me, I'm weakening!

THE LADY

There!
I liked you better than the other one
From the very moment I laid eyes on you.

THE DISCIPLE

O Master, I can do penance afterwards!

THE LADY

(Excitedly)
Penance? Of course you can!
(Picking up the undervest)
I've brought the very thing!
It's lined with my own hair, it's really delicious!
I meant it as a present for him, but I'll give it to you!
Hair-shirts are penance, aren't they?

THE SWAMI

Put that penance down!

THE DISCIPLE

(Clutching the undervest)
Master, it's too late! I sway, I swoon!
A woman's hair! There's madness in the moon!

THE LADY

I haven't much, but what I have is mine!
That's only in a shirt.

THE DISCIPLE

(Clasping her head to his breast)
Yours is divine!

THE SWAMI

(Rising in terrible wrath)
Madman, back to your prayer!

THE DISCIPLE

There's madness in the moon! A woman's hair!

THE SWAMI

(Reaching into a basket)
Then die!

THE DISCIPLE

(On his knees)
Oh, Master, Master, I'll be good!

THE SWAMI

Not till you're dead. Go, cobra, take your food!
(With a cobra he stings the DISCIPLE, *who crumples and falls.)*

THE LADY

You shall pay dear for this! By God, I swear!

THE DISCIPLE

(Moaning into death)
There's madness in the moon! A woman's hair!

THE SWAMI

That man was a curse in India.
I was the only saint in India
Willing to let him beg with me.

THE LADY

A curse?

THE SWAMI

It began when he was eight. He found his nurse
Asleep one day and gathering all her hair
Into his little fists, he pulled. She almost died.
And ever since that melancholy day
The Rajah of Majalapur has tried
To cure his son of this unnatural sin.
Before he came to me, they had had to pay

Eleven million rupees to the kin
Of women who had lost their heads of hair—
Because of that young fellow lying there.

THE LADY

How terrible!

THE SWAMI

Yes, wasn't it! You're right.
No girl in India went out at night,
And none by day without a quaking fear
Lest she return naked from ear to ear.

THE LADY

(Her hands to her head)
Would he have—?

THE SWAMI

Yes, by the roots.

THE LADY

What an escape!
And I never dreamed of anything but rape.

THE SWAMI

Asleep he dreamed of hair and even dead—

THE LADY

Why did he do such things?

THE SWAMI

He was overbred.
Too many years of wealth and of Oxford three.
He was overcivilized. Now look at me—
Always a Brahmin, always a gentleman.
Give me the shirt and watch me put it on.

You see how easily it fits my soul?
Come close and let me prove my self-control.
Come closer, closer, let me put my hand
Into your bosom, calmly, you understand.

THE LADY

Let me alone, you horrible thin old thing.

THE SWAMI

(With great scorn, to the returning PASSERS-BY)
See what she brought us as an offering,
Bowls of jade and cups of rhinoceros-horn!

A PASSER-BY

In love with the Disciple?

A SECOND

Her dress is torn.

A THIRD

(Seeing the body)
Look! He's been murdered!

THE SECOND

I must tell my wife,
She'll be delighted.

THE FIRST

But a life's a life.

THE LADY

(To the SWAMI)
Say that you did it with a cobra!

THE SWAMI

No.
You did with a shirt!

THE LADY

It isn't so!
You don't believe him, please, you don't, you can't.

THE THIRD PASSER-BY

I must go and tell my sister.

A FOURTH

I must go and tell my aunt.

THE SWAMI

(Rising)
Leave her alone with him—
Punishment fitted
Precisely to the crime that she's committed.

THE FIRST PASSER-BY

(Gazing at the corpse, almost in tears)
Grandmother always liked him. She was called
His first offence. She was completely bald,
But she always liked him. She was the famous nurse.
She isn't well and this will make her worse.
Poor grandmother.
   (The PASSERS-BY *gather the articles of beggary and start away.)*

THE LADY

You're taking all my clothes and all my food!

THE SWAMI

Nothing is anyone's but solitude—
And death.

THE LADY

My blouse!

THE SWAMI

Nothing is yours.

THE LADY

(Desperately clutching at a last veil)
It is!

THE SWAMI

(Wresting it from her)
First meditate—then try that shirt of his.
    (They all leave, taking everything but the dead DISCIPLE'S *garment. After a moment the* LADY *covers her bare shoulders with it. Then she approaches him, looks into his face and lifts his head against her bosom.)*

THE LADY

Lay your head quietly upon my breast.
You loved me. I was different from the rest.
I know I could have cured you of your craze,
You were so charming in all other ways.
You should have been my love. In fact you shall!
I shall but live as your memorial.
What an experience! What a romance!
No other woman ever had a chance
To carry in her heart what I shall carry.
I shall be faithful. I shall never marry.
If only he had known enough to sham,
If only he were feigning death!

THE DISCIPLE

I am!—
I dodged the snake and tumbled like a clod!
    (Glaring)
I'm ready for you, Lady!

THE LADY

O my God!
>   (*She lifts her skirt and flees headlong, the* DISCIPLE
>   *following.*)
>   (*Darkness.*)
>   (*The music from Salome, that accompanies the beheading of
>   John the Baptist.*)
>   (*Light reveals the* LADY *on the Height, lying in bed,
>   exhausted. She wears an enormous multi-coloured wig.
>   Servants are fanning her, and the* UNICORN *is offering cake.*)

THE UNICORN

The wig is beautiful. Don't moan.
It's an improvement over your own.
Why should you weep, Lady, why should you care
For a little thing like loss of hair?

THE LADY

From an Asian fever!

THE UNICORN

Think how few
Could go through all that you've been through.

THE LADY

>   (*Still moaning*)

I feel as though I had swallowed the world,
And could never be purged!
Vitality is what I need!
Bring me vitality!

THE UNICORN

The glands! What ho!
>   (*He strikes the gong.*)
>   (*Four* SERVANTS *enter, bearing two large balloons.*)

THE LADY

(Weakly)
You should have ordered me a smaller size.

THE UNICORN

Lady, I ordered you perennials.
Once they are on, they sprout of their own accord.
There's nothing like the spring agglandizement.
(The LADY *swoons.)*

THE UNICORN

Poor little bunch of sea-weed, pushed ashore,
Uneasy in the sun,
Trying to bore
Into the sand with roots, when roots there are none!
(To the SERVANTS*)*
Attach them.
(The SERVANTS *attach the balloons to her like water-wings.)*

THE LADY

(Sitting up)
Better already. Give me a piece of cake.
(Receiving it from the UNICORN*)*
I am coming back to life, and, Unicorn,
I see all my experience in a purple flash
As drowning people do. One who has lived
As rich a life as I have, Chinese lovers,
Artists in Paris, Swamis, even cannibals,
Ought to become a public character.
Autobiographies have been too tame.
Bring me my pen and let me tell the world
The things that ought to be autobiography.

THE UNICORN

(Striking the gong)
Paper and pen and ink, her signature!
*(*SERVANTS *go for them.)*

THE LADY

(Selecting from the cake-dish)
I can tell fortunes by shuffling lady-fingers
Or by studying the lines of a macaroon.
I can see the future by gazing through a doughnut.

THE UNICORN

(Holding a doughnut between her eyes and the audience)
What do you see?

THE LADY

(Considering the audience and shaking her head)
Superior souls are far apart in the world.
You can always tell by gazing into a doughnut.
   (To a SERVANT *entering with the vermilion pen)*
Give me the pen.
   (Obeying awkwardly, the SERVANT *pricks one of the
   balloons, which explodes, whereupon the* LADY *falls back
   moaning.)*

THE LADY

O Unicorn, a gland, another one!

THE UNICORN

(Shaking his head)
Pituitary of a mastodon?
We stole these two from the Smithsonian.
There are no more, unless a monkey-gland—

THE LADY

Hurry! The blood is ebbing from my hand!

THE UNICORN

(With abrupt candour)
These were not glands, only balloons. We lied.

THE LADY

    (Gasping)
You should have told me sooner. I might have died.
I may be dying now for all you know,
Something is wrong with me and hurts me so.
If only I were as dead as the mastodon!
Is it too late for me to be a nun?
    (She collapses.)

THE UNICORN

She's sinking. I don't like this in the least!
    (Striking the gong)
Bring, every one of you, a cake of yeast.
    (One of the SERVANTS *runs out.)*

ANOTHER SERVANT

But yeast has been prohibited!

THE UNICORN

Now come!

THE SERVANT

They've found that it's a stimulant, like rum.

ANOTHER SERVANT

And several of our neighbors are in prison.
It was discovered that their bread had risen.

THE FIRST SERVANT

    (Returning breathless, with large yeast-cakes)
The undertaker's opened a blind pig!
He's brought us yeast-cakes in a funeral-rig!
    (They feed the LADY.*)*

THE UNICORN

She's rising! Rising! Venus from the foam!

THE LADY

(Sitting up, rubbing her eyes)
Have I gone west?

THE UNICORN

No, Lady, you've come home.

THE LADY

(Easily)
And now, my Unicorn, my pet,
Bring me a perfumed cigarette.
   (As he does so)
I shall begin my book this afternoon
With the final chapter, "A Gland or a Balloon."
Then I shall write it backward, Chinese fashion,
To an early chapter, "Burial of Passion,"
And how I touch the heart of a Hindu mystic
And make a negro nobly atavistic,
And how my libido has been released
By nature's remedy, a cake of yeast!
Only a woman like me could have known from the first
That to yield to the senses is to be accursed.
Another cigarette.
   (The CAKE-SERVANT *brings her one. She notices him again.)*

THE LADY

Oh, what a joy.
To have for a servant such a pretty boy!
Bring me a match, bring me a tray.

THE UNICORN

   (Aside, while the CAKE-SERVANT *obeys)*
Every Unicorn has his day.
   (Sotto voce, to another SERVANT*)*
Have we no better uses than to linger

Beside a lady with a lady-finger?
(*Consulting a time-table from his pocket*)
A taxicab! Grand Central Station.
(*He begins a Charleston step toward the exit.*)

THE SERVANT

(*In the same tone, and joining, behind him*)
Shall you be taking a vacation?

THE UNICORN

Taking my coat, taking my hat,
Taking a cab, and after that—
Taking a train, the 2:23.

THE SERVANTS

(*Whispering, and joining; in groups of two*)
And me! And me!—and me!—and me!
(*To their Charleston lock-step and music, fingers on lips, they all leave, followed by the* CAKE-SERVANT, *without her noticing.*)

THE LADY

(*Nonchalant, superior*)
The fool hath said in his heart, "There is no cake."
This is a beautiful world, there's always cake.
I want some cake. Bring me some cake.
(*No one comes. She looks behind her to the right and to the left. She looks again. Still no one comes. There is no cake. Oh, there is, for at this moment, the* CAKE-SERVANT *returns, with a smile.*)

THE CAKE-SERVANT

The others have all left you.

THE LADY

The Unicorn?

THE CAKE-SERVANT

Out on the sidewalk, blowing his own horn.
I'm staying.

THE LADY

Good. You have a spiritual look.
You shall become Custodian of my Book.
There's no great difference, is there, in our ages!

THE CAKE-SERVANT

There were eight of us. Do I get all the wages?

THE LADY

(Indicating the cake-dish)
I want one.

THE CAKE-SERVANT

(Bringing it)
What? A doughnut?

THE LADY

Maybe so.
(She takes one, and considers him through the opening.)

EVE

(Appearing for a moment and prompting from the side)
Why don't you marry him, Lady?

THE LADY

I don't know.
(With sudden zest)
We'll have a grand reception, dear, and show
The social world that you are comme il faut.
What are you, anyway?

THE CAKE-SERVANT

(Boldly helping himself to cake)
I'm hungry. See?

THE LADY

Your ancestry, I mean, your family-tree.

THE CAKE-SERVANT

(Hopefully)
I had an uncle, steward on a steamer.

THE LADY

(Resolutely)
You are a Russian nobleman, a dreamer!

THE CAKE-SERVANT

But I'm a Pole.

THE LADY

Be quiet! Let me speak.
You are descended from a royal Greek.

THE CAKE-SERVANT

(Plaintive)
But I'm a Pole.

THE LADY

A nobleman, that's certain.
I'm going to be a Countess. Pull the curtain.
(The Height is curtained.)

THE LADY

(Thrusting her head through the curtain and handing out a packet of envelopes)
Ring for a messenger.
(As he does so in the air)

And then invite
The people whom we had that Friday night
When I entertained the Baron and the Duke
And the multimillionairess from Dubuque.
   (She withdraws her head.)

A MESSENGER

(Entering with a Social Register)
Next time you send your bids out, ask for me.
I got a book here that'll help you, see?
A list of the swells, and I got the real ones checked.
   (Taking the envelopes)
Are these to go prepaid?

THE CAKE-SERVANT

No sir. Collect.
   (Calling off-stage, opposite to the MESSENGER'S *exit)*
Hey, get a move on, bring along the chairs.
Come in your shirtsleeves, fellows. She's upstairs.
   (To quick jazz music in a quick jazz figure, stagehands set on the lower stage a semicircle of eight chairs with four chairs, symmetrically spaced, behind them.)

THE CAKE-SERVANT

(Motioning each invisible person to a seat)
The guests! Miss Hare, Mrs. Bacon. Mr. Fox. Mr. Wolf.
   Miss Catt.
Dr. Stork and both the Lyons. You can sit down where you're at.
   (As four members of the orchestra start to follow)
No, you don't, you fellows. Where's your invitation?

LEADER OF THE ORCHESTRA

(Carrying a trombone)
We don't need any. We're the conversation.
   (They take the four seats in the second row, with trumpet, trombone, clarinet and oboe.)

(The curtains part. The LADY *enters in a tea-gown, her wig wound close about her head with tulle and orange-blossoms. She shakes hands with an invisible person in one of the front-row chairs.)*

THE LADY

How good of you, Miss Catt, to come!
(When the player behind Miss Catt has made a cattish answer)
You say my announcement struck you dumb?
I doubt it, dear.
(Moving on to the next empty chair)
And how do you do!
It's Mr. Lyon—and Mrs. too.
(When the trombone has roared a gruff remark and the oboe squeaked an apologetic syllable)
I know, Mrs. Lyon, but he has to be rude.
It's his genius—and he's always so charming with food.
(Moving on with her handshakes)
Mr. Fox, once again on the scent, I suppose.
There's nobody has so successful a nose.
And here's Mr. Wolf in the very next chair
To the charming, retiring and gentle Miss Hare.
(When Messrs. Fox and Wolf have made instrumental advances to Miss Hare, who sits between them)
Dr. Stork, I'm so glad you prescribed me that diet.
Why don't you persuade Mrs. Bacon to try it?
(Looking about for the CAKE-SERVANT, *while her friends converse, finally seeing him flattened against the proscenium arch and crossing to him)*
They're here!
Substantial New Yorkers, all of them, dear.
(Turning to them)
The handsome young husband I want you to meet!
He's from Poland, a Count, he's a darling, he's sweet.

THE CAKE-SERVANT

(Hanging back as she takes his hand)
I've changed my mind. O Lady, please!
If you only knew how I hated teas!
I shouldn't have done it.

THE LADY

(Severe)
A pretty affair!

THE CAKE-SERVANT

I can't go through with it.

THE LADY

Come, be square.
(With a resolute inspiration.)
Will you let the toss of a coin decide?

THE CAKE-SERVANT

(Piteously)
Lady, I'd rather not be tied.

THE LADY

(Dominant)
No sir. The coin.
(Demanding one out of his pocket)
On this depends
Whether you marry me.

THE CAKE-SERVANT

(Moaning)
You and your friends!

THE LADY

It may cost me a Count, but I've counted the cost.

THE CAKE-SERVANT

(Slapping the coin on the back of his hand)
If it's heads, I win.

THE LADY

(Looking)
It's tails. You've lost!
(She conducts him to greet the substantial New Yorkers, while the conversation soars loudly into the Mendelssohn Wedding March.)

FINAL CURTAIN

GUEST BOOK

· ❧❧❧ ·

[1 9 3 5]

Apology

Here are my guests recorded in a book
And noted not with an invidious eye;
For I have tried to concentrate my look
On certain essences I know them by,—
Nothing inimical, nothing adverse
Nor friendly, nor considerate, nor kind,
But honesties, for better or for worse,
Concerning both the body and the mind.
And if it seem that I have paid a cost
Too dear for decency, too bad for me,
I may have gained as much as I have lost
By the direction of my scrutiny:
Though I can claim no virtues that I sign,
These faults are nobody's that are not mine.

Blue Book

The Blue Book states her stature, but it blurs
In her own eyes before a midnight mirror.
The height is someone else's and not hers;
Adam and Eve made an immortal error.
She's on all fours before herself tonight,
Addressing other monkeys' images.
The mirror shows a colonel on her right
And on her left a lawyer, both of these
Grinning like apes, disguising bare behinds
And picking up their forks with hairy fingers.
Despite their monkeyhood they may have minds,
But somehow it's the monkeyhood that lingers.
"Cage or a jungle, which am I in?" she cries.
Her answer is a pair of beady eyes.

Charioteer

Here is a woman whom a man can greet
Equal to equal, which is something said;
For seldom will a man forego conceit
And grant a female room, till she is dead.
But here's a woman different: a young mind
In a body aging with no age at all.
She's like a living portrait whom you find
Some rainy night in your ancestral hall,
The spark within her eye aware and human. . . .
Having Athena's mind, Achilles' heel,
She's mythological, this modern woman.
Torn from the chariot, a loosened wheel
Which kept the chariot upon its course,
She runs ahead, beyond the fallen horse.

Communist

How happily he flaunts the newest flag,
Its heraldry the hammer and the sickle!
Though not quite knowing if it's just a rag
Like ordinary flags not worth a nickel,
He waves it in a dream, foresees a race
Divorced completely from the dollar-sign
And with ideals illuminates his face.
He deems the Russian people half-divine
Because they happen to live far from here,
Thinks every one of them a superman
And acts amongst us as a Paul Revere
Ringing awake whatever bell he can.
The shot around the world is coming back!—
His neighbours merely read the almanac.

Or else they say unfriendly things about him:
Some element is missing from his life.
While to his face they half-politely flout him,
Behind his back they criticise his wife.
If she sufficed the man, would he go hunting
Across the world for fevers of the brain?
Hammer and sickle may appear a bunting
And yet be bandages for private pain.
Some of his neighbours are less kind than these,
Fiercely accounting him a public foe;
And others let him ramble if he please;
He may be right, they say, for all we know.
And so he watches in the daily press
For more to happen, though it's only less.

Debutante

A debutante at birth and ever since,
A wiser child than Henry James's Maisie,
She has, with eyes that very seldom wince,
An unwise voice, occasionally hazy
From too much knowledge and from too much gin,
From too much resolution to be gay.
Lightly she touches every modern sin,
But sin has never touched her, so they say.
She asks about it, if it's worth the price,
She flirts with every manner of suggestion,
Coquettes with every whispering of vice;
But meantime it's a more than open question
If the whole world have anything to offer
Of vice or virtue to the little scoffer.

Dorian

He assumes the Morris chair, for Dorian
Forgets that comfort was Victorian.
Upholstered in his ease, he puffs the smoke
Of a jaded super-futuristic joke.
He hails the style of anyone who writes
However dully about stalagmites,
Provided stalagmites are other things
Than stand in caves. He thinks that borrowings
Are favours granted by an easy spender;
And if there's dunning, he believes the lender
Ought to be crucified along with Jesus.
Thereupon, having spent the thirty pieces,
He gives away his underclothes and hats
And ties his throat to a fig-tree with cravats.

Dowager

Cutting her skirt too short, her swathe too wide,
Coupons too often, capers now and then,
She wears her years like diamonds to hide
Her ancient nakedness from modern men.
Clucking out syllables of majesty,
Tiara-sentences and ermine-wit,
She never wholly manages to be
More than herself nor less, no, not a bit.
White-haired and central, she commands her world
Like Genghis Khan himself commanding slaughter,
And on her right and left, superbly pearled,
Sit her adjoining daughter and grand-daughter,—
As though the Trinity had changed its sex
And wore the change upon three female necks.

Expatriates

Rossetti might have quarreled with Burne-Jones
To be the father of so fair a lad;
But a manufacturer of candy owns
The fathership, wishing he never had.
He knows that nothing in his own good strain
Accounts for the full lips and the wild ways,—
It's something for the mother to explain;
She's had it on her conscience all her days.
Regardless of the cause, the boy continues
Between his loves to paint (or almost never),
Trusting his eyes and curly hair and sinews
Beyond the need of study and endeavour,
Until in Paris he has found requital:
An Englishwoman with a worn-out title.

She pounced upon him, so they say, like Jove,
Liking his cherub face and fleshy wings.
And he liking her force. And then they clove
Together, circling through the airy rings
Of Paris, not an eagle and a boy
But a hawk and a rabbit, or a dead balloon
And a broken parachute, or a paper toy
Caught on a telegraph-pole, or a yellow moon
And a wisp of cloud. As long as they had brandy,
Their very bed was wafting through the ether
A mother of liquor and a son of candy;
But lacking this refreshment, they had neither
Paris nor anything. It was no joke:
They were dry as hell and both of them dead broke.

Ghost

He rises from his guests, abruptly leaves,
Because of memory that moons ago
Others now dead had dined with him, and grieves
Because these newer persons he must know
Might not have loved his ghosts, his unknown dead.
There are new smiles, new answers to his quips;
But there are intervals when, having said
His dinner-table say, he hears dead lips . . .
The dead have ways of mingling in the uses
Of life they leave behind, the dead can rise
When dinner's done; but one of them refuses
To go away and gazes with dead eyes
Piercing him deeper than a rain can reach,
Leaving him only motion, only speech.

Gourmande

Wishing to have a will, she wills a wish
That has no more to do with will than when
The eddy of a current turns a fish
And then as idly turns it back again—
Except that malice never actuates
The watery shifting of a spotted trout,
Unless an appetite for worms and baits
Happen to be the thing that, looking out
For life, takes life as well. She is not that.
Her appetites are empty after all.
Though she is fed and surfeited and fat,
She does her best to drink a waterfall—
Not that she wants the water for a minute,
But she thinks she had better be round it than be in it.

Harlemite

Summer transforms her from her evening-suit
And drapes a satin blouse about her fat,
In which she settles like a parachute
Upon her evening club. The eyes of a cat
Glance from her head toward her white customers.
She purrs among them, barely bothering;
And yet if an untoward event occurs,
She can go on and move, go on and sing
And wield a whip withal in her own way.
Tip of her tongue and bosom of her basso
Can coin obscenity and seem at play
And yet can turn like a Brazilian lasso
And swing around a neck she doesn't like:
The rattlers curl and the constrictors strike.

Jeremiah

Roses have been his bed so long that he
Constructs a mat of thorns for lying on;
People have flattered him, until the sea
Becomes a preferable monotone.
He sets his masonry upon the brink
Of lamentation, out of his window peers
Toward waves that ever rise only to sink
Confused and lost as he among his years.
A ship alive becomes to him a hull
Charred and undone, the fumble of a wreck;
His dreams are but the droppings of a gull
Caught in a noose of seaweed round his neck;
And crying like a maniac toward the sky,
He pulls mankind in after him, to die.

Mayflower

Although on Beacon Hill he's hurried after
By proper debutantes and satellites,
Liquor and lapses, lecheries and laughter
Are the alliteration of his nights.
He has an honoured name, yet hopes it true
(Despite the family furniture and fuss)
That he was only, in the Mayflower crew,
A seaman able and anonymous,—
A brawny fellow excellent at sailing,
Fond of his muscle, fond of hearty fun,
Fond of his bedfellows and good prevailing
When all the thoughts and theories are done.
And so on any night in any street
He sails abroad, enamoured of a sheet:

A sheet that winds to him a lovely limb
Away from family warranties and crests
Which hold no such significance for him
As the important heraldry of breasts.
And so he waits the coming of the night
To be less honoured but more understood,
To find upon a curb uncurbed delight;
He'd certainly be happy, if he could.
He eyes the younger company at home
(Disarming both his parents by his speech)
As 'twere a chorus at the Hippodrome
With not a girl or boy beyond his reach.
And yet the sail he craves from early seas
Lacks in his handling the propitious breeze.

Noblesse

In a town of nondescript and easy folk
She is boasting always of her coronet,
Until the thing becomes a village joke,—
A velvet gown a village dog has wet.
To every legend that she tells, the town
Adds many lighter memoirs in such haste
That the deep design of jewels in her crown
Become a jolly pyramid of paste.
And while she thinks she motors out in state,
Seen by the town as its especial glory,
The townsmen only wonder that her mate
Can listen to her everlasting story . . .
Although her ancestors be extra fine,
It's not her lineage, it's just her line.

Pedagogue

He picked a pathway leading from a shelf
Outdoors and in, back to the books again,
And philosophically deceived himself
That he could people paths with docile men
And women, could apply them to his pleasure,
Could take his tranquil trousers off and trip
With boys and girls any impetuous measure,
Then turn to Dante for companionship.
These unrealities were let alone
To prosper among kindly elements,
Till the wind one night took off its monotone
And hurricaned a music too intense
For one who thought that passion was no rocket
But just a simple candle in a socket.

He who had planned his candle as a light
To lighten Gentiles in the outer dark
Became Egyptian, Philistine, Hittite,
Roman and Hebrew, mingled in one bark;
And such a complicated sap went through
The ringed fibres of his graceful trunk
That instantaneously branches grew
Out of his midst, and every twig was drunk;
And so he locked his wife in a bedroom closet
Among the garments he had seen her wear
And gave his own inordinate composite
A most luxurious chance to take the air,—
No sooner done than, heavy with contrition,
He joined his wife behind the same partition.

Philosopher

Accosting circumstance with a good line,
He takes his hat off to the future, sets
His tie and ventures forward with a fine
Disdain of all misgivings, all regrets.
He knows the best of the philosophies
Because, intuitive, he understands
That life is just exactly what it is
Despite mismanaging ambitious hands,—
Is what it was and shall be and is now.
To him, despite all words of tongue or pen,
Life's mainly the exaggerated bow
Which any rooster makes to any hen:
Religion passes and the age of reason,
But sex is everlastingly in season.

Poetess

She was as callous in the execution
Of verse as though of Sacco and Vanzetti.
She knew the academic convolution
Which gives immense importance to the petty.
She would have ordered God from the front door,
If he had come in clothes that meant the back.
Her rights had been her rights so long before,
She deprecated wrongs and, leaning back
With her fastidious mind, would burn fat logs
And drink her Turkish coffee and forget
The breed of anarchists. A breed of dogs
Fawned at her knee expectantly, to whet
Her self-importance with less violent jolts
Than come to zealots from electric volts.

Spouse

Now this Ophelia was a wiser woman,—
She wanted all his life and all his worth;
And yet she said, Since he is only human,
I can lie down upon my lonely earth.
I can allow him Tuesdays, if he chooses,
To stay away from me and let me nurse
My sentimental madnesses and bruises.
I have six days of him. It might be worse.
The others come, the others go, she said,
But I can madden only upon him.
So let me moan, along the river-bed,
That he is absent from the river-brim
And weave these flowers in my hair for sorrow,
For this is Tuesday,—Wednesday is tomorrow.

Stylist

He had a face from Michigan, a mask
Of blue-eyed innocence and beardless satin,
And so primarily he made his task
The adapting of his dimples to Manhattan
But went too fast, adding Parisian gleams
And little twinkles of uncertain sin
And even took upon his face the seams
And less adroit appearance of Berlin.
Later of course, and it was rational,
His paunch and visage both assumed a look
Not national but international
In spite of all the purgatives he took;
And while his titles gathered on the shelf,
The man became fictitious to himself.

Teacher

Teacher of boys—and yet afraid the rule
Of lordliness in class should come besides
To be a habit and he play the fool,
He has a look which what it half confides
It more conceals. He flutters on the verge
Of telling you, first with his eyes and hands,
Then nearly with his tongue; and yet the urge
Is less than something else which countermands.
Therefore his conversation turns to dreams
And their interpreting or to some such case
Of Freudian theory. A flicker gleams
Of almost rabid fervour on his face
And in his voice there's an excited tone—
Toward other people's cases than his own.

Tragedienne

She chose to be an actress long ago
And so continues to the bitter end,
Not knowing now, nor will she ever know
The role that she intended to intend.
She picks the book up, as she used to do
When it was stage, and sees herself appear
Before an audience, herself and you,
And weighs the ultimatum of a tear.
But whether this play or the other play
Or still a third contain the better part
She cannot answer any more today
Than when the question first troubled her heart.
She puts the volumes back upon the shelf
And has no part to play except herself.

Wormwood

All she can talk about is who was who
In various branches of her family tree;
All she can think about is never you
But only and interminably she.
And so the countless wrinkles on her face
Have come from stiff assertion of her pride,
From putting other people in their place,
Below the place of people who have died
Bequeathing their importance to herself
And their dead dust to her undying mouth.
She spies the family bible on a shelf,
Becomes the flood, the locusts and the drouth,
All seven plagues that Egypt suffered from.
She may be deaf, but she is never dumb.

Her lineage seems to make the wrinkles darker
Than they have need to be upon a brow;
Her skeleton seems visible and starker
Than common vertebrae concerned with now.
She enters with a rustle of old bones,
Not hers nor anyone's; for out of place,
Denied their honest quiet under stones,
The dead go yet unburied in her face.
They haunt her gestures dankly with concern
And punctuate her speech with periods
Of chilly pause and make her every turn
Seem like a wormy motion under sods.
If only she would lay her down and die,
The dead might be at peace and so might I.

THE DEATHLESS LAUGHERS, THE FORGOTTEN GODS

· ✥❈✥ ·

SELECTED VERSE

[1 9 0 7 – 1 9 5 4]

Processional

The rain has ended. Tiny moths and swallows
And poising dragon-flies flit one by one
Before a long processional that follows
Of all the dynasties under the sun.
I watch the Mongols and the Tartars pass;
The Mings, the Manchus and the Japanese;
And then the Europeans; and then, alas,
Even Americans go by like these.
And other shadowy forms before my eyes
File along twinkling willows into space:
Leaving the swallows and the dragon-flies
And tender moths and me to run our race
Light-hearted, at the ends of periods,
With the deathless laughers, the forgotten gods.

Be Not Too Frank

Be not too frank, if you would reach
A woman's heart, be not too kind
Nor too severe, but keep your speech
And all your manners uninclined.

Assert but briefly self-control;
Then watch her come to you intent
To give direction to your soul
And make indifference different.

The South

     O the true difference!—
The sun at last
Gilds me again
And my face is no more a white stalk of celery
But a golden mango
And the foot-tracked mud of my heart
Is sunk deep down
In the blue waters and purified with a scouring
Of coral. . . .
Cranes carry peace to the east and the west
And joy stands clear by the mangroves,
A torch,
A flamingo.

The Fire-mountain

Forget you?—
Can that Hawaiian volcano
Forget its quick fountains and cascades
Of fire?

The Canyon

It is the dead sex of the earth
On which the sun still gazes.

It is all the mountains of love,
Into whose sarcophagus
Peers
The moon.

Crystal

Between your laughter and mine
Lies the shadow of the sword of change.

Yours is innocent.
Mine knows

You had sat abstracted
By the touch of dreaming strings
Of an old guitar—
When in the centre of the room
A crystal dish cracked for no reason.

Then you darted with joy to the fragments,
Like a fish to a crumb,
And held between your thumbs and your fingers
Two pieces of laughter.

Divertisement

1. I GAMBLE

I threw the dice with Death,
I won.
Again I won.
Death only smiled . . .

But so did the deep-bosomed toad,
And the birch
Winked its pencilled eyes.

2. I EVADE

The look in your eyes
Was as soft as the underside of soap in a soap-dish . . .

And I left before you could love me.

3. I WONDER

In my desert of familiars
Time rocked like a camel under me,
Ungainly, heaving minutes,
Shaggy hours,
Four feet gathering into a season,
Trailing into years . . .

O sullen-swaying ship,
Is this difference the shadow of palm-trees?—
Or only the shifting of my familiars,
The sands?

4. I DRINK

Wine is a worship . . .
Blue peas
Are set in rows
In pods of lapis lazuli
When gods eat,
And though oysters
Are white as dawn and singing
From the sea—
The hearts of humming-birds
Are black as a storm
In summer.

5. I LAUGH

Now when embers whisper
And mice cry in the wall
And a chair in the dark crosses its legs—
I am thinking of one
Of whom I shall not be thinking some later night
When embers exclaim
And mice laugh in the wall
And the chair in the dark uncrosses its legs.

Episode of Decay

Being very religious, she devoted most of her time to fear.
Under her calm visage, terror held her,
Terror of water, of air, of earth, of thought,
Terror lest she be disturbed in her routine of eating her husband.
She fattened on his decay, but she would let him decay without pain.
And still she would ask, as she consumed him particle by particle,
Do you wish me to take it, dear? Will it make you happier?
And down the plump throat he went day after day in tid-bits;
And he mistook the drain for happiness,
Could hardly live without the deadly nibbling. . . .
She had eaten away the core of him under the shell,
Eaten his heart and drunk away his breath;
Till on Saturday, the seventeenth of April,
She made her breakfast on an edge of his mind.
He was very quiet that day, without knowing why.
A last valiant cell of his mind may have been insisting that the fault was not hers but his;
But soon he resumed a numbness of content:
The little cell may have been thinking that one dies sooner or later
And that one's death may as well be useful. . . .
For supper, he offered her tea and cake from behind his left ear;
And after supper they took together the walk they always took together after supper.

Ghost

I died the other night and, dead,
Chose to be a cat
And returned to my own funeral, shed
Of both my coat and hat.
And neither hat nor coat
Appeared on any mourner.
Naked from toe to throat,
They showed me in my corner
That only their clothes had cared,
Only their words could grieve.
And because they all were bared,
I wanted much to leave
And was just about to go
When a woman they thought to ignore
Stood apart as though
With tears at every pore.
So back again I came to her
And I brushed by at her feet.
She leaned and stroked me on the ear
And the touch of her was sweet.

The Four Senators

(Tell it to the Marines!)

They took a little voyage, combining it with rest,
A business expedition to the islands of the blest.
And, having sailed the Caribbean to hear what they have heard,
They now urbanely testify that the Eagle is a bird,
A mighty but not flighty bird, of lineage and loin,
A bird upon the seal of state, a bird upon the coin,
A paragon of eagles, never a bird of prey.

(There were some German eagles, only the other day.)

The State of Poetry, 1954

```
        not
they do     like sense in poetry any more
        not
nor nonsense either
just posture
they are intent upon
      s         r
p           U         y
   o                t
         t       i
let them have it
```

A Great Man

Passion transforms me from my puny build . . .
Your bosom listens to me like a crowded balcony
To a great man speaking.

The Wanderer

Sometimes when people pity me
    I tell them with no rancor
That for what it costs me to be free
    I might have bought an anchor.

Housecleaning

We opened an unopened drawer
And found what we had found before,
Neckties with patterns out of date
And other minor toys of fate—
And a sudden portrait of us two
When you were I and I was you.

Arthur and Louise

Arthur and Louise
They met one day,
Arthur and Louise
They met one day,
And she said to her man,
"You goin' away?"

And Arthur he answered,
"You're nothin' but a nut,"
And Arthur he told her,
"You're nothin' but a nut,"
And Louise she answered,
"I may be—but—"

And Louise she rolled
The edge of an eye,
And Louise she rolled
The edge of an eye,
And they both got to die,
We all got to die.

A Bird That Sings

Unless we remain children, we grow too old.
So buy a toy with me in the market-place,
A bird painted singing on a dish of clay,
Or a water-bottle to hang on a firefly,
Or a basket for a beetle to market with.
What would a market be like, unless we were children
Prizing above all else a bird that sings
Within this dish of clay, this human breast?

Poems for Children

TURKEY-COCK

He was like father, yes, he was,
    His face was red as fire,
He puffed the same way father does
    And tried to stand up higher.

He tried to say important things
    That father tried to say.
You know how father thumps his wings
    At mother every day?

PELICAN

Old Aunt Matilda was there in the Zoo.
Though they called her a pelican, everyone knew
That there couldn't be two of her, one in a cage
And the other at home with a newspaper page.

I used to run back, as fast as I could,
But somehow she got there ahead and she stood
With her nose looking down and her foot in a shoe,
Just as life-like at home as she was in the Zoo.

A TRUANT

I take off my hat to the mountain
And I take off my shoes to the pool;
For moments come seldom to count in
Away from the counting at school.

There are seventeen mountains, three cows and
Two pools and a cottonwood tree
Which, added, make ten hundred thousand,
Though a teacher would say twenty-three.

Where the brook shoots across like a fountain,
There's a very good place to keep cool;
So I shout off my shirt to a mountain
And I shake off my doubt in a pool.

A trout is my shadow-companion,
The sand is like gold to my toes . . .
O, it's easy to learn in a canyon
As much as the principal knows!

The Storm-Dragon

1

A water-snake trailing lily-bulbs,
Or a rattler slowly coiling on Tunapec. . . .
But where is the winged serpent all the while?
Has he coiled his spirit away on pyramids? . . .
With the oxen and burros we hide our frightened eyes.
We have seen him coming through a gap of hills,
Throwing a horseman down, overturning a boat,
His horizontal plumage stiff with rain.

2

He huddles us aside out of his way,
He breathes on us, he drowns us with his breath,
He burns our eyes with his, he claps his wings
Over our heads. Longer than a mountain,
He passes and passes, miles of him in the wind.
And afterwards the dragging of his tail
Has slashed the roadway to a yellow froth
And spun the meadows whirling at their trees.

Dans Cette Galère

I
Yes, he was like that:
A piece of paper flying,
Brown paper flying
Over high copings and water-tanks
Against fire-escapes and at windows,
Now and then sheer for a moment
Above them all,
A brilliant brown thinness,
A piece of paper flying,
Brown empty paper flying
Across the enormous blind eyeball of sky.

II
I saw last night a woman:
She had a calf as clean and shapely
As meat unsheathed from a lobster-claw
And yet, alas, never unsheathed
Since her soul was the claw.

III
Whether a yes or a no were spoken,
The difference, being only between her own breasts,
Gave her no comfort
And her mouth had the curve of a lemon-peel
Thrown away after drinking.

IV
Children of jade
Had hardened his happiness
Into something less than a heart.

V
Though she carried no bowl of milk,
The hills and valleys followed her like cats.

Fingernail

He had a fingernail which resembled the face of his grandmother
Who had died in her dignity before he was born
And had bequeathed her slim grace to only one of his fingers.

So he chose long moments during the sunsets
For polishing this one nail delicately and meditating
Upon what was left him of the persistent earth.

An Old Colloquy

I love you.
Yes?
Do you love me?
No.
Is it someone?
Yes.
Who loves you?
No.

Master of Moons

Along the Havana wharves was a sugar-train—
And an iron black, unloading bags from it,
His torso bare, with valleys of wet muscle,
His rhythm sure as that of tigers pacing.
And across from the car was a house of many women,
Two of them quarrelling, a black with a yellow,
And the little yellow woman swung her palm
Agàinst the black cheek of her adversary
Who, towering massive as a mountain-side,
Let loose an avalanche of angry might.
And they fought and blazed, and each of them tore off
The other's only garment, whirling in bronze,
Till out from the sugar-car black waters leapt
And lifted the giantess to a naked shoulder
Like a great log along a stream at midnight
And carried her away into the distance.

Li Po before the Emperor

Here I am, drunk again,
Li Po, drunk again.
How can I, drunk again,
Sing for Your Lady?
There are You, high again,
Heaven's Son, high again.
How can I try again
Still to hold steady?
Here am I, late again,
Facing my fate again.
Why must I state again
Words with a brush?
How can my soul again
Feel itself whole again?—
Hand me the bowl again!
Everyone, hush!
Words will come down again,
Birds will come down again,
Thrushes be brown again—
Almost I hear them.
No, they're away again.
How can I stay again
Things I could say again
If I were near them?
Pour me the bowl again!
Let me be whole again!
Tether my soul again
Close to a wing!
Now they are there again,
Blown through the air again,

Now I can dare again,
Now I can sing,
Now I can fly again,
Before I die again,
Now I can sigh again,
Sigh with delight!
Here goes my brush again.
Everyone hush again . . .
There came the thrush again.
Lady, good-night.

The Edge

Long, long before the eyelids harden
And an intake ends the breath,
A body's eyes and a body's burden
Feel the edge of death.

They do not move, they do not think,
They only sit and stare,
The eyes almost ceasing to blink
And the heart ceasing to care.

But it becomes a pleasant thing
To gaze upon the toes
So peacefully dismembering
Before the eyelids close.

Thus Buddha must have sat and known,
Midmost of earth and sea,
The dissolution of the bone
Into its rarity.

A Winter Cat-Tail

Cat-tail standing in the ice,
Elderly New Englander
Standing mirrored in the ice,
Thin straight stalk and ruffled fur,
Do you wonder where the wind has blown
Dandelion and golden-rod?
Or are you happier alone
With the loneliness of God?

Epitaph for a Constant Lover

He encountered new mistresses most of his life,
Though—if better were lacking—he lay with his wife.
Now he lies with his latest—from falling downstairs—
Eternally constant, and nobody cares.

NEW
POEMS

[1960]

And that was all
    Said the duckling
    Without closing his bill
    Which was caught by surprise
    In the middle of some other sentence
    Than always happens
    When the web leaves the foot
    Unexpectedly
    And stays away
    So much of the time

And that was it
>The preternaturally small cave
>Into which creatures crawled backward
>Without sufficiently asking where or when
>Which of course is why

Because her hand hung over the edge of the bed
    It was bitten by something like a fish
    With an undershot shiny jaw
    And with a welcome smile
    Which would not have been there otherwise

But for these apertures
    Said the turtle
    Man would not have lost
    The address of the gods

    He hid it in here
    In my shell
    And I have had no use for it
    Yet

A circular den it is
    But bounded from left to right
    Which saves it from too much circularity
    When it runs from right to left

    And at its very center
    Sits a spider
    As great upon occasion
    As anyone needs to be
    With its circular den inside out
    And its attenuated part
    Delivering the ultimatum

    Of such tender silk
    Are our brains woven
    And our women
    Given to taking out of the belly
    And into it again
    All so snug
    The silken silent universe
    And the buzz
    Of a bluebottle planet

The dress walked in by itself
    But with the greatest dignity
    As though what was not inside
    Greatly mattered
    Even the other day

    And that after all was what made the occasion

The foot came through
    In spite of all the pressure under it
    For the water was there where it should be

    But in the end
    The telescope prevailed
    By bringing back the one star
    Shining only up

Furniture has feet too,
> The bed the chair the sofa
> But they walk away beyond distance
> More kindly than people do
> More slowly

The greatness of laughter
    Outdoes all other kinds

    How animals try for it
    If you could see them in the dark
    But they find crying there so much easier
    Or just noise
    Not yet mirth
    The greatest of noises
    A melted snarl
    A bark
    Exalted

He never knew what was the matter with him
    Until one night
    He chopped up his bed for firewood

    It was comfortable that way

    And then another night a year later
    It came roaring up the street at him
    As a sunset

He noticed from the dark shore
    That it was his own house being carried awkward on the flood
He could see by the unlit lights in the living-room
That it was filled with total strangers
Dancing
And that the flooring of a flood
Is at an angle

He replied that it was not so
    And she agreed that it was
    Which is more or less what it would have been
    Without their comment

He was not always there
    But he tried to be
    He was constantly looking for small objects
    Where he had not left them
    Or repeating remarks he had not made
    So that people's eyes went back and forth over him
    Like tennis balls over a net

    It was not that he felt in the least tied down
    But that a part of him was elsewhere
    Like the holes in the net

Hundreds of times
    The sloth would walk across my door-sill
    But solely to remind me
    That its head was too small for its body

    And I could only help thinking that if the world were that polite
    It might do
    At least on occasion

If I could let go and swim through time
    I might reach an unsuspected end of it

    But it is an acrobat
    Facing either way
    And if I pass it one way
    It turns the other

    Judges as well as athletes forget that time runs back
    Faster than forward

Important in the bar-room
    At nine o'clock
    Because the bar was there and he still standing
    He put his feet on the ceiling as he had never failed to do
    Before
    But somehow it seemed strange to him
    This time

It happened that she turned on the light
    Just as the fence disappeared
    Leaving only its gate
    So that the crowd could not pass
    But stood there
    Helpless and lowing
    So that even the bull was turned about
    Where the sun rose the other way

I think I'm on the floor when I'm not

    Of course feet make better speed
    When they advance on no substance
    Move only in air

    But one little slip
    And they can be drowned in firmament

    How happy the remotest bird
    Coming into touch again
    With almost anything

It made speed
    But on its antlers
    Instead of its feet

    No horns were speedier than those
    Especially when turned to the left

    And it stood there
    Guarding its young
    Upside down
    As was only natural
    Under such conditions

    And with the icicles

It was his jaw that was wrong said the doctor
    It could not keep from laughing

    So it had to be broken and mended
    Which was done
    Without mending the laugh

    Psychiatrists shook their heads at him
    But only one came off

Just as we had prepared all outdoors
    For the elephant
    He brought a third ear into the house
    And laid it on the bathroom floor
    For a mattress
    So that only one of the three walls was left standing
    And only the opening of the doorway
    Without anything around it

    And even then he could not manage coming through
    To the rest of the house
    In spite of his not having yet been in it

    So he gave up
    And left in two directions
    Without preferring either

    Until dark

Might we not go to sleep now
    With a mountain of the moon guarding us

    It would be a comfortable a sweeter sleep
    Than that of moles
    Who are asleep already
    Or of owls
    Who can shut only one eye
    Or the bats
    Who cannot use the night properly
    Except on those occasions
    When all lightnings combine
    And even tadpoles walk precociously with thunder

    But all the sleep has been spoken for and in the rain
    Months earlier

    And sleep was easier then
    When nobody was left alone
    When there was at least somebody in the other room
    But now there is nobody anywhere

Now comes the crocodile with sealed eyelids
    Walking asleep
    Armored against nightmares
    But with a dream in every limb

Once upon two times
    It happened
    And everybody saw double
    But recognized
    The reality
    As separate

The only disadvantage unsolved
    Is caring
    And yet not caring is more difficult in the long run

    If one could confront
    The face of care
    In a mirror
    And then suddenly flip the glass over
    And leave only one face
    On the back of it

She was taking her child to be repaired
    And said to me
    Why do they break so easily

    But it was the child speaking
    And I hardly answered

The steamer-rug
    All of a sudden
    Stood its contents upright
    A dozen feet from her chair
    And whirled her about toward the edge

    But I could do nothing
    Because there was no other chair
    Vacant

There the swallows come
　　Flying backward
　　Following their tails

　　It makes all the difference in the world
　　Cries one of them
　　Swinging his tail forward like a cleft halberd
　　And capturing something
　　Longer than a beetle
　　And less useful

Think of all those nights
    When the other body was more your own
        than your own was

    And yet here you are
    And here is yours
    More itself than ever
    Turning from side to side
    Both commonplace

Those rows of curving seats
    Are my ribs
    The actor said
    In which my heart sits
    And the hands clapping are its beats
    Which somewhere in the darkness
    Would become quiet arms
    If they could only reach me
    On such lonely occasions

To this witch
> At last the world was clear
> With the snow intact
> Under the soil
> With pelicans thick on the ice
> And penguins in the air
>
> Her haunch was as full of clarity at noon
> As her heel had been at midnight

The tragedy of being larger than you are
   Is endless
   But since it is impossible to be smaller
   Why try

   Unless you have someone
   Who begs you not to
   While looking at you through the wrong end
     of the opera-glass
   And in public

Two slender oysters
    On a spring walk
    Gossiped once
    Out of their shells
    And with pearls on leashes

Under a light he hid his bushel
    And wondered
    When it did not burn
    Why he had not done otherwise

    Or at least
    The opposite

Up from sea-bottom
    Through my pillow
    But slowly

    Its peak felt first
    Because coming deepest

    Slow angular iridescent
    As though the midnight-sun were captured
    In this freedom under sea

    And then up up
    Up through my warm marrow

    The whole iceberg

Voices in the staircase
    In the floor
    In the furniture

    There are more of the dead here
    Than of the living

    Except for the voice
    Which sometimes comes through
        passionately
    I do not wish to be born

When in the spray
    The future appears
    It trails the past
    Then twirls into itself
    And becomes a ring
    In a forgotten ear

Yes I hear them
> Steps on the staircase outside my door
> With no one attached

> I have stopped looking
> But always when I snap off the last bulb
> The footsteps come and wander

> And always
> When the dawn-light follows
> They wander away
> Footsteps with no one attached

> I have stopped looking
> So that last week
> They changed
> They came with the daylight and are here now

> But we have no railings

You fish for people and not even their names
    Come up for you

    But the sun is still there
    Aged fisherman
    And you sit in it fishing for people
    And hooking the sun